THE COTTAGES OF ENGLAND

Frontispiece PLATE C

Cottages by the Church at Westham, Sussex
From a Water-colour by E. Leslie Badham, R.B.A.

THE COTTAGES OF ENGLAND

A REVIEW OF THEIR TYPES AND FEATURES FROM THE 16TH·TO THE 18TH·CENTURIES

By
BASIL OLIVER F·R·I·B·A
Author of ~ "Old Houses & Village Buildings of East Anglia

With a Foreword By
The right Hon. STANLEY BALDWIN, MP

This edition digitally re-mastered and
published by JM Classic Editions © 2007
Original text © Basil Oliver 1929

ISBN 978-1-905217-49-6

All rights reserved. No part of this book subject
to copyright may be reproduced in any form or
by any means without prior permission in writing
from the publisher.

". . . I shall not neede (like the most part of Writers) to celebrate the Subject which I deliver. For Architecture can want no commendation, where there are Noble Men, or Noble Mindes; I will therefore spend this Preface, rather about those, from whom I have gathered my knowledge; For I am but a gatherer and disposer of other mens stuffe, at my best value . . ."

". . . In Architecture as in all other Operative Arts, the end must direct the Operation. The end is to build well. Well building hath three conditions Commoditie, Firmenes, and Delight . . ."

[From *The Elements of Architecture*, " collected by Henry Wotton, Knight, from the best Authors and Examples," published in London, in 1624.]

FOREWORD

IT has always seemed to me, as it must, I think, to anyone who has been brought up in a home amidst some of the most beautiful old cottages of England, that it is difficult to contemplate such fine examples as appear in the illustrations of this book without realizing that the whole of this architecture is one of the tributaries of the main stream of mediæval craftsmanship that has come down to us at our time. As such, these old cottages are of inestimable value to-day. They have an appearance of spontaneous and natural craft which is fully lacking in those abortions of red brick and slate which have arisen with such alacrity over the face of the country since the industrial era began. It is an education in itself to see the adaptation of local means to the meeting of local needs, and the excellence of local craft in a village, say, in the Cotswold country or the South Downs of Sussex.

While we all recognize that good housing is, and ought to be, a great civilizing power, we have to confess that we and our immediate ancestors have neglected it both from that point of view and from every other point of view. Neglect always has to be paid for at great price, and the neglect of the past two or three generations is being paid for to-day in hurry, and, too often, in want of thought. William Morris once said that it was his function to stain wallpapers with poetry. No one can say that we have stained buildings with poetry for the last two or three generations. We have stained them with prose, and pretty bad prose at that.

Now the problem, as I understand it, is that we want to preserve old houses, but not simply as curiosities. We want to bring them back into the main stream of national life. We want to see them made adequate for the needs of people to-day. We believe that can

FOREWORD

be done, and we believe it would be a most valuable lesson. We want, as wise people always do, to take a *via media* between, on the one hand, that type of brutal despoiler who is never happy unless he has lodged himself in a vulgar villa that is an eyesore to the countryside, and, on the other hand, the kind of fanatic who is a fanatical restorer and who pins his faith in a spurious antiquity. We want neither of these things. We want the middle course, and we want to enlist in our support an enlightened public opinion, without which progress is impossible. It is having regard to this fact that all those of us to whom the old rural architecture means so much, and in whose lives it has played so great a part, find a source of comfort in the fact that a society such as the Royal Society of Arts should have taken this subject seriously into consideration in the movement it is organizing for the preservation of the old cottages of this country.

Mr. Basil Oliver has been called upon to write this volume by his fellow members of the Executive Committee of this movement. It should be a welcome one for enthusiasts, for its illustrations demonstrate more competently than any amount of propaganda ever could the vigour of design, and suitability for their purpose and setting, of the types of old cottages still to be found in all parts of the country. For the indifferent and cynical it will, I think, be something of a revelation; and I can only hope that it will find its way into the hands of as many as possible of those who have to do with the maintenance, preservation or erection of cottage buildings throughout England, whether they be architects, builders, landlords, or just ordinary folk.

Stanley Baldwin.

PREFACE

IT might easily be supposed, in looking through the illustrations contained in this book, that all is well with rural England. Unhappily this is not the case, although it must be admitted that this country is still rich in characteristic examples of beautiful old cottages.

They are, however, a diminishing quantity, sometimes through indifference, narrowmindedness or vandalism, but more often through lack of money to stay otherwise preventable decay.

Hence the movement by the Royal Society of Arts for their preservation by means of a Fund to be subscribed for that worthy purpose.

This book was the natural corollary, and it has been produced in the hope that it will tend further to stimulate interest in our wonderful heritage of the vernacular peasant homes of our ancestors, and incidentally to swell the somewhat limited subscription list.

The growing national consciousness of the vandalistic dangers constantly threatening our countryside was given expression by the former Prime Minister, the Right Honourable Stanley Baldwin, M.P., when he presided at the inaugural conference called by the Royal Society of Arts on January 26, 1927, and, as Chairman, he proposed a resolution approving the action of the Society, and signifying the intention of the meeting . . . " to assist in the establishment of a substantial fund for application on the broadest national lines in furtherance of this movement."

PREFACE

Chief credit is due to Sir Frank Baines, K.C.V.O., C.B.E., F.R.I.B.A., as the actual inspirer of the Society's new activity, as well as to its Secretary, Mr. G. K. Menzies, M.A., for his unflagging enthusiasm. Both have the cause genuinely at heart.

The very remarkable collection of photographs of cottages, accumulated in the course of years by the late Mr. Herbert Batsford, and continued by his nephew and successor, Mr. Harry Batsford, Hon. A.R.I.B.A., was a very powerful factor, apart from the natural fascination of the subject, in influencing me to attempt so formidable a task.

Messrs. Batsfords' prints have formed the nucleus of my illustrations, and though the process of sifting and bettering my selections has gone on continuously for over a year, quite a large number have sufficient merit to have remained unaffected by the changes and eliminations.

With such a wealth of material it has been considered desirable to restrict the scope of this book to England alone, and to eschew farmhouses, almshouses, and inns, etc., and to illustrate only cottages or buildings of purely cottage type.

No two persons could agree as to which are the best examples in any one county. Tastes vary, and there are so many different points of view. I make no such claim for my final choice, but I have endeavoured, as far as possible, to be impartial between the pictorial and the architectural interests, and to select for my plates buildings exhibiting most markedly regional traits adequately representative of each and every county, so that anyone who is familiar with rural England can more successfully name the locality to which they belong.

I am indebted to the Royal Photographic Society of Great Britain for their courtesy in granting me the privilege

PREFACE

of inspecting, before exhibition, the photographs submitted in connection with their Annual Competition, the subject of which for 1928 was an old English cottage or group of cottages. In this connection also I have to thank Mr. Thomas H. B. Scott, Past-President, and Mr. H. H. Blacklock, the Society's Secretary.

Plate 47, from a photograph at Trotshill, by Mr. Arthur J. Woodley, and Plate 91, at Tong, from another by Mr. Edgar R. Bull, F.R.P.S., were awarded plaques, as the two best exhibits. From the same source came Mr. W. H. A. Fincham's photograph, Ickleton (Plate 66) and one by Mr. Percy S. Hudswell (Plate 55), Ravensden.

Three of my Huntingdonshire examples (two on Plate 62 and one on Plate 64) are reproduced by permission of the Royal Commission on Historical Monuments, and were selected by me from a collection of over 2,200 photographs (the gift of Mr. E. J. Horniman to the Victoria and Albert Museum) especially taken, but only in part used, for the Commission's volume on that county.

The frontispiece is from a water-colour painting (exhibited in the Royal Academy Summer Exhibition of 1928) by Mr. E. Leslie Badham, R.B.A., to whom and to its owner, the Rev. Sidney Swann, I am grateful for the loan of the picture, and for their ready permission to make a colour-block from it.

Mr. Eric Maclagan, C.B.E., F.S.A., the Director and Secretary of the Victoria and Albert Museum has sanctioned the use of my drawing made from a print from the official negative of the quaint old wrought iron inn-sign (Fig. 32), formerly at Huntingdon, but now in the Museum at South Kensington.

Mr. Sydney R. Jones has kindly permitted me to use Geological Map (Fig. 1) from *The Village Homes of England*, written and illustrated by him and published by *The*

PREFACE

Studio in 1912. The Map is now reproduced by the courtesy of the Editor, as also are Mr. Alfred H. Powell's drawings (Figs. 8, 9, 10, 11, 19, 35, 36 and 37), which were made for and used in the *The Studio Year Book, 1920*. I have also to acknowledge the permission of the Director-General of the Ordnance Survey Office to reproduce two plans of villages (Figs. 2 and 3).

I am beholden to Mr. A. Whitford Anderson, F.R.I.B.A., for my Hertfordshire illustrations (Plates 52, 61 and 81) and for generously giving me numerous other photographs of cottages in that county; to Mr. E. J. May, F.R.I.B.A., for the use of his measured drawings (Figs. 12 to 18 inclusive) of Vine Cottage, Kenilworth; to Mr. Alfred H. Powell for the loan of his drawings, in pencil and in ink, from which many of my letterpress illustrations (Figs. 5 and 6, 8 to 11, 19, 27, and 35 to 38) have been made, either direct or from ink-line tracings of them, as well as for his helpful interest in my searches and researches; to Mr. Nathaniel Lloyd, O.B.E., F.S.A., for allowing me to use his photographs (Plates 48, 59 and 78), for the photograph from which my drawing (Fig. 21) was made, for lending me three carefully drawn details of casement-fasteners (Figs. 29, 30 and 31), specially made for him by Mrs. Dorothy Buckmaster, and for his kindness in showing me how amazingly rich in architectural treasures are the counties of Kent and Sussex, in the locality of his beautiful home, Great Dixter, at Northiam; to Mr. W. J. Harrison, the Bursar of Clare College, Cambridge, for the use of his Madingley photograph (Plate 61); to Mr. Sydney Pitcher, F.R.P.S., of Gloucester, for giving me the benefit of his intimate knowledge of the Cotswold district, and for his exceptionally good photographs (used for Plates 1, 28, 29, 30 and 46); to Mr. Robert Chalmers, F.R.P.S. (for Plate 69); and to all the other skilful photographers whose names are given in the index of Plates. From their work I have freely drawn, and I would particularly single out for commendation the following :—Messrs. B. C. Clayton; Herbert Felton, F.R.P.S.; F. Frith & Co., Ltd.; George Hepworth; and Will F. Taylor. I have also used some excellent examples of the well-known photographic work by the late Mr. W. Galsworthy Davie and by the late Mr. Taunt, of Oxford, from Messrs. Batsfords' extensive accumulation.

Delightful as pencil, ink, or colour sketches of old cottages may be, there is always a temptation to the artist to restore, or omit, with the result that there is more risk of disappointment later on when the actual subject of the picture is seen. A good photograph, however, has the compensating value of greater reliability, and for this reason I have consistently favoured photographic representation in spite of many temptations to depart from it.

My obligations would by no means be complete without one final word of gratitude to Mr. Harry Batsford for the trouble he has taken in assisting me, without stint, to obtain only the best photographs of the most representative subjects, and, having procured them, then taking infinite pains to extract perfection out of the reproductions, often a great deal better than their originals.

But I had long known of the thoroughness of the House of Batsford, from previous happy experience.

BASIL OLIVER.

ERRATA

Preface, page x, 2nd para.
For *Tong* read *Limpsfield*.
For *Ickleton* read *Lavenham*.

CONTENTS

	PAGE
QUOTATION	v
FOREWORD. By The Right Hon. STANLEY BALDWIN, M.P.	vi
PREFACE	viii
LIST OF PLATES ARRANGED UNDER NAMES OF COUNTIES	xv
LIST OF ILLUSTRATIONS IN TEXT	xxi

INTRODUCTION

The Preservation of Old Cottages and the desirability of their retention for those for whom they were built—Old Building Methods and Advice by Contemporary Writers—The Development of the English Cottage——External Charm and lack of Internal Convenience—Landlords—Geological Influences and Local Characteristics—Aerial Photographs and Village Plans—Typical Village, Landscape and Street Views. . 1

CHAPTER I. STONE-BUILT COTTAGES

Poor foundations of early types—Cornish granite-building—Traditional position of chimney in Somerset—Admixture of flint in bands and chequerwise in Wiltshire and Dorset—Cotswold Types—Examples of Devon, Somerset, Dorset, Wilts., Glos., Worcs., Berks., Oxon., Yorks., Derbyshire, Northumberland, Leicestershire and Northants. Cottages 19

CHAPTER II. TIMBER-FRAMED COTTAGES WITH STUDDING EXPOSED

The various Types and Regional Characteristics—Skill and Knowledge of the Old Carpenters—Methods of In-filling and Finishing—Representative Examples from different parts of England . . . 27

CONTENTS

CHAPTER III. TIMBER-FRAMED, CLAY LUMP, COB AND STONE COTTAGES, PLASTERED EXTERNALLY

Composition of old plaster—Ornamental Pargetting—Essex "Stickwork," Pricked and Combed Patterns—Clay Lump—Cob and Stone with plain Whitewashed Surfaces—Examples 42

CHAPTER IV. TIMBER-FRAMED AND PARTLY BRICK-BUILT COTTAGES, TILE-HUNG AND WEATHER-BOARDED

Mostly found in Kent, Sussex and Surrey—Illustrations from these three South-Eastern Counties 55

CHAPTER V. BRICKWORK AND FLINTWORK

Renewed use of bricks after timber became scarce—Revival of brickmaking in 15th and 16th centuries—Influence of Great Fire of London on popularity of bricks—Paucity of good examples—First introduced in Eastern Counties—Some East Anglian types of brick and brick-and-flint—Foreign influences in Norfolk and Suffolk—Larger size of bricks during period of brick tax—Survival of flint mining and knapping from prehistoric times—Brick-and-flint Gables—Chimneys of East Anglia compared with those in South-Eastern group of counties—Brick-and-stone cottages—Examples of different uses of brick from Herts., Norfolk, Suffolk, Lincs., Yorks., Glos., Hants., Bucks., Dorset and Wilts. 60

CHAPTER VI. FEATURES AND DETAILS

Chimneys—Slate-hanging and other weather-resisting precautions—External Staircases—Doorways—Windows of different types—Wrought Ironwork—Glazing—Gardens, and old writers on their Charm—Dry-walling and Thatched Walling—Thatch, its advantages and disadvantages, methods, and necessary precautions—Advice by old and modern writers 71

INDEX 87

ALPHABETICAL LIST OF PLATES
ARRANGED UNDER NAMES OF COUNTIES WITH NAMES OF PHOTOGRAPHERS

BEDFORDSHIRE
	PLATE
Maulden. Herbert Felton, F.R.P.S., London	63
Ravensden. Percy S. Hudswell, Bedford	55

BERKSHIRE
Ardington. The late H. W. Taunt, Oxford	57
Blewbury, Thatched Wall. The late H. W. Taunt, Oxford	99
East Hagbourne. B. C. Clayton, Ross-on-Wye	93
Hampstead Marshall. The late W. G. Davie	96
Steventon. The late W. G. Davie	50
Steventon. The late W. G. Davie	51
Steventon. The late W. G. Davie	94
Steventon. The late W. G. Davie	94
Sutton Courtney. The late W. G. Davie	49
Theale. The late W. G. Davie	95
Woolstone. W. A. Call, Monmouth	32

BUCKINGHAMSHIRE
Bishopstone. F. R. Yerbury, Hon. A.R.I.B.A., Arch. Assocn.	60
Bishopstone. F. R. Yerbury	60
East Claydon. F. R. Yerbury	53
Quainton. F. R. Yerbury	87
Simpson. Herbert Felton, F.R.P.S.	53
West Wycombe. The late W. G. Davie	95

CAMBRIDGESHIRE
Barrington. W. C. Rayner	65
Ickleton. B. C. Clayton	66
Madingley. W. J. Harrison, Cambridge	61

CHESHIRE
Allostock. Fred H. Crossley, F.S.A., Chester	41
Nether Alderley. Fred H. Crossley	93
Swirres Eye. Fred H. Crossley	41

CORNWALL
St. Ives. Will F. Taylor, London	90
Sennen, Cottage showing the Tablemên. Gibson & Sons, Penzance	19
Sennen, Cottage near Beach. Gibson & Sons, Penzance	19
Tintagel, Old Post Office. Gibson & Sons, Penzance	20

ALPHABETICAL LIST OF PLATES

CUMBERLAND

	PLATE
Ruthwaite, John Peel's Home. G. P. Abraham, Ltd., Keswick	10

DERBYSHIRE

Beeley. T. E. Routh, Derby	9
Eyam. F. Frith & Co., Ltd.	39
Higham. T. E. Routh	9

DEVONSHIRE

Coombe Cellars. F. Frith & Co., Ltd., Reigate	71
East Budleigh. Valentine & Sons, Ltd., Dundee	16
Honiton. W. E. Berry, Honiton	70
Landkey Newland. The late W. G. Davie	92
Lee, Herringbone Stone-Walling at. F. Frith & Co., Ltd.	99
Lustleigh. F. Frith & Co., Ltd.	22
Salcombe Gullet. F. Frith & Co., Ltd.	15
Yealmpton. The late W. G. Davie	36

DORSET

Bridport. F. Frith & Co., Ltd.	24
East Lulworth. F. Frith & Co., Ltd.	14
East Lulworth. F. Frith & Co., Ltd.	71
Melbury Abbas. B. C. Clayton	24
Morden. B. C. Clayton	86
Puddletown. A. E. Walsham, London	25
Shaftesbury. B. C. Clayton	13
Studland. F. Frith & Co., Ltd.	32
Swanage. The late W. G. Davie	37
Wareham. Aerofilms, Ltd., Hendon	3

DURHAM

Wearhead, Co. Durham. Valentine & Sons, Ltd.	10

ESSEX

Great Dunmow. H. Dan	65
Great Warley Street. Robert Chalmers, F.R.P.S., Sunderland	69
Newport. H. Dan	18
White Notley. F. Frith & Co., Ltd.	17
Witham, Chipping Hill. F. Frith & Co., Ltd.	17

GLOUCESTERSHIRE

Bibury, from the Square. B. C. Clayton	4
Bibury, near Arlington Row. B. C. Clayton	4
Bibury, Arlington Row. Sidney Pitcher, F.R.P.S., Gloucester	28
Bibury, Arlington Row (a near view). Sidney Pitcher, F.R.P.S.	29

ALPHABETICAL LIST OF PLATES xvii

PLATE

Calcot. Sidney Pitcher, F.R.P.S.	1
Chedworth, View of the Village. B. C. Clayton	6
Chedworth, Row of Cottages. B. C. Clayton	6
Childs Wickham. Percy Simms, Chipping Norton.	7
Ebrington Hill. Sidney Pitcher, F.R.P.S.	30
Frampton-on-Severn. G. Granville Buckley, M.D., Bury, Lancs.	49
Frampton-on-Severn. G. Granville Buckley, M.D.	85
Kilcot, Old Cider Mill. B. C. Clayton	99
Lower Tuffley. Sidney Pitcher, F.R.P.S.	46
Sevenhampton. B. C. Clayton	31
Stanton. B. C. Clayton	31

HAMPSHIRE

Fleet. Nathaniel Lloyd, O.B.E., F.S.A., Northiam	48
Godshill, Isle of Wight. F. Frith & Co., Ltd.	16
Kettlebrook. F. Frith & Co., Ltd.	50
King's Worthy. The late W. G. Davie	87

HEREFORDSHIRE

Eardisland. B. C. Clayton	13
Pembridge. Will F. Taylor	43
Pembridge. Herbert Felton, F.R.P.S.	43
Pembridge. Will F. Taylor	55
Vowchurch. B. C. Clayton	42

HERTFORDSHIRE

Aldbury. A. Whitford Anderson, F.R.I.B.A., Watford	52
Hadham Ford. A. Whitford Anderson, F.R.I.B.A.	81
Walkern. A. Whitford Anderson, F.R.I.B.A.	61

HUNTINGDONSHIRE

Alconbury Weston. Aerofilms, Ltd.	2
Brampton. F. Frith & Co. Ltd.	63
Hilton. } The Controller of H.M. Stationery Office (Royal Commission on Historical Monuments)	62
Holywell.	64
Sawtry Judith	62

KENT

Chiddingstone. Harold H. Camburn, Tunbridge Wells	58
Elham. Nathaniel Lloyd, O.B.E., F.S.A.	59
Groombridge, The Green. Harold H. Camburn, Tunbridge Wells	74
Groombridge, The Walks. Harold H. Camburn	74
Groombridge, The Walks (another view). Harold H. Camburn	74
Groombridge, The Blue Cottages. Harold H. Camburn	78
Hawkhurst. The late W. G. Davie	79
Smeeth. The late W. G. Davie	73

xviii ALPHABETICAL LIST OF PLATES

LANCASHIRE

	PLATE
Hawkshead, Flag Street. F. Frith & Co., Ltd.	88
Hawkshead, External Stairs, etc. F. Frith & Co., Ltd.	88

LEICESTERSHIRE

Hallaton. T. E. Routh	40
Newtown Linford. T. E. Routh	52

LINCOLNSHIRE

Frodingham. F. Frith & Co., Ltd.	84
Scrivelsby. H. Walker, Louth	72

LONDON

Hampstead, North End Cottages. W. Whiffen	77

MIDDLESEX

West Drayton. The late W. G. Davie.	58

NORFOLK

Bawburgh. B. C. Clayton	81
Bawburgh. B. C. Clayton	80
Happisburgh. Thomas Lewis, Ltd.	83
Heacham Green. F. Frith & Co., Ltd.	82
Wreningham. B. C. Clayton	64

NORTHAMPTONSHIRE

Harlestone. The late W. G. Davie	96
Wicken. B. C. Clayton	40

NORTHUMBERLAND

Alnwick. Valentine & Sons, Ltd.	11
West Boat. Gibson & Son, Hexham	39

NOTTINGHAMSHIRE

Normanton-on-Soar. T. E. Routh	54
Sutton Bonington. T. E. Routh	54
Sutton Bonington. T. E. Routh	54

OXFORDSHIRE

Finstock, Post Office. The late W. G. Davie	34
Great Tew, Cottages. The late W. G. Davie	35
Great Tew, Cottages (another view). The late W. G. Davie	35
Thame. The late W. G. Davie	51

RUTLAND

Barrowden. Dolby Bros., Stamford	12
Empingham. Dolby Bros.	12
Stretton. Dolby Bros.	12

ALPHABETICAL LIST OF PLATES

SHROPSHIRE

	PLATE
Hopton Castle. B. C. Clayton	44
Tong. Will F. Taylor.	91

SOMERSET

Allerford. F. Frith & Co., Ltd.	23
Bratton. F. Frith & Co., Ltd.	14
Dinder. The late W. G. Davie	34
Nunney. F. Frith & Co., Ltd.	27
Selworthy. F. Frith & Co., Ltd.	21
Westford. F. Frith & Co., Ltd.	36

STAFFORDSHIRE

Abbots Bromley. T. E. Routh.	42

SUFFOLK

Flatford. Will F. Taylor	68
Flatford. S. A. Driver, Ardleigh, Essex	85
Glemsford. Charles F. Emeny, Sudbury	67
Kersey. S. A. Driver	18
Lavenham, Lady Street. G. Ranson, Lavenham	56
Lavenham, Water Street. Will F. Taylor	56
Lavenham, Water Street (another part). W. H. A. Fincham, Hornsey, N. 8.	66
*Little Cornard. Charles F. Emeny	67
South Cove. B. C. Clayton	80

SURREY

Brewer Street, Bletchingley. The late W. G. Davie	73
Chiddingfold. The late W. G. Davie	75
Frensham, Cottage Garden. The late W. G. Davie	97
Great Bookham, Cottage Gardens. F. Frith & Co., Ltd.	97
Limpsfield. R. S. Ponting, Anerley, London, S.E.	76
Limpsfield. Edgar R. Bull, F.R.P.S., Brockley Road, S.E.	91
Nine Elms, Milford. The late W. G. Davie	77
Witley. Herbert Felton, F.R.P.S.	76

SUSSEX

Mayfield. The late W. G. Davie.	75
Northiam. Nathaniel Lloyd, O.B.E., F.S.A.	78
Tillington. The late W. G. Davie.	92
Westham, from the Water Colour by E. Leslie Badham, R.B.A., St. Leonards-on-Sea	Frontispiece
Whatlington, on the road to. The late W. G. Davie.	79

* These cottages have since been repaired.

ALPHABETICAL LIST OF PLATES

WARWICKSHIRE

	PLATE
Dunchurch. F. Frith & Co., Ltd.	45
Stoneleigh. B. C. Clayton	44
Wixford. F. Frith & Co., Ltd.	45

WESTMORLAND

Hartsop, Spinning Gallery. G. P. Abraham, Ltd., Keswick	89

WILTSHIRE

Castle Combe. F. Frith & Co., Ltd.	5
Castle Combe. F. Frith & Co., Ltd.	5
*Fisherton-de-la-Mere. (The late) H. Brooks, Salisbury	26
Hudswell. F. Frith & Co., Ltd.	27
Lake. Herbert Felton, F.R.P.S.	86
Potterne. Valentine & Sons, Ltd.	48

WORCESTERSHIRE

Broadway. Herbert Felton, F.R.P.S.	33
Cleeve Prior. F. Frith & Co., Ltd.	72
Elmley Castle, A Cottage Garden. W. A. Call	98
Little Comberton. Arthur J. Woodley, Worcester	47
Norton. Herbert Felton, F.R.P.S.	46
Trotshill. Arthur J. Woodley	47

YORKSHIRE

Beck Foot. George Hepworth, Brighoute	37
Bolton Percy. George Hepworth	84
Kilburn. George Hepworth	38
Osmotherley. George Hepworth	7
Runswick. Valentine & Sons, Ltd.	8
Sandsend. F. Frith & Co., Ltd.	8
Sutcliffe Wood. George Hepworth	38

*NOTE.—With reference to Plate 26 of Fisherton-de-la-Mere, in the Wylye Valley of Wiltshire, to the North-West of Salisbury, it should be stated that since the photograph was taken, some thirty to forty years ago, the whole of the front wall of the charming cottage on the right has been rebuilt.

Unfortunately the flint and stone chequer-work disappeared in the process, and windows needlessly inappropriate were substituted for the pleasant three-light windows of the original front, and a stone arch was put over the doorway whose pointed head is seen to be formed with bricks, in the plate.

The church in the background is not now so fully exposed to view since trees have grown up.

That Constable recognised the picturesque value of this unusual and entirely happy composition is indicated by the fact that he is supposed to have introduced it as a background for a picture he once painted of sheep-washing, though there is no record of any such picture in the Victoria and Albert Museum, nor in any book or photograph, illustrating Constable's work, in the Museum Library.

There is also nothing like the subject of the plate amongst Sir Robert Witt's remarkably comprehensive data.

INDEX TO ILLUSTRATIONS IN TEXT

ALPHABETICALLY UNDER COUNTIES

FIG.		PAGE
1.	England, Geological Map of (Sydney R. Jones, *d.*)	9

ESSEX

28.	Saffron Walden, Early Seventeenth Century Wrought Iron Casement, now in Victoria and Albert Museum, from (See also under London) (B.O. *d.*) .	74

GLOUCESTERSHIRE

6.	Tunley, Cottage (demolished 1919) at (Alfred H. Powell, *d.*)	24
5.	Tunley, Ground Floor Plan of Cotswold-type cottage (Fig. 6) at (A. H. Powell, *m.d.*)	23

HUNTINGDONSHIRE

32.	Huntingdon, Eighteenth Century Wrought Iron Sign Bracket, now in the Victoria and Albert Museum, London, from (See also under London) (B.O. *d.*) .	76

KENT

23.	Broadstairs, Diapered Gable in High Street at (J. P. Seddon, *d.*)	63
20.	Chiddingstone, near Edenbridge, External Plaster Treatment on a cottage at (B.O. *d.*)	45
21.	Mereworth, Maidstone, Seventeenth Century Pargetting on a Fifteenth Century building (now cottages): an example of pressed scroll ornament near (B.O. *d.*).	46
26.	Smarden, Detail of chimney-capping at (B.O. *d.*) .	66
26.	Tenterden, Details of typical Kentish chimneys at (B.O. *d.*)	66

xxii INDEX TO ILLUSTRATIONS

FIG.   PAGE

34. Tenterden, Detail (partly conjectural) of eaves-treatment on Seventeenth Century brick-built Guest-house (now cottages) at Finchden, Appledore Road, near (B.O. *d*)   78

33. Tenterden, Ornamental lead-glazing in Guest-house (same as Fig. 34) at Finchden, Appledore Road, near (B.O. *d*.)   77

LONDON

28. Victoria and Albert Museum, Early Seventeenth Century Wrought Iron Casement from Saffron Walden, Essex, now in the   (See also under Essex) (B.O. *d*.) .   .   74

32. Victoria and Albert Museum, Eighteenth Century Wrought Iron Sign Bracket from Huntingdon, now in the   (See also under Huntingdonshire) (B.O. *d*.) .   .   .   76

28. Victoria and Albert Museum, Wrought Iron Casements from Suffolk, now in the   (See also under Suffolk) (B.O. *m.d.*)   74

30. Victoria and Albert Museum, Enlarged details of fasteners
31. to same, now in the (Dorothy M. Buckmaster, *m.d.*) .   75

28. Victoria and Albert Museum, Wrought Iron Casement from Godalming, Surrey, now in the   (See also under Surrey) (B.O. *m.d.*)   74

29. Victoria and Albert Museum, Enlarged detail of fastener to same, now in the (Dorothy M. Buckmaster *m.d.*) .   75

NORFOLK

35. Bacton, near North Walsham, Reed plait instead of laths, tied to rafters under thatched roof at (A. H. Powell, *d*.)   83

24. Potter Heigham, Measured detail of gable-end at (the late John S. Corder, *m.d.*)   64

24. St. Olaves, Old Cottage at (inset on Potter Heigham elevation) (the late J. S. Corder, *m.d.*) .   .   .   64

SOMERSET

36. Isle Abbots, near Taunton, Fence at side of dormer against thatch at (A. H. Powell, *d*.)   .   .   .   84

37. Isle Abbots, Thatch over window at (A. H. Powell, *d*.) .   85

INDEX TO ILLUSTRATIONS

SUFFOLK

FIG.		PAGE
25.	Great Cornard, near Sudbury, Brick chimney-stack (probably late Seventeenth Century) on Mill Tye Cottages at (B.O. *d.*)	65
3.	Hartest, near Long Melford, Plan of (Ordnance Survey)	13
4.	Kersey, from the North (B.O. *d.*)	17
22.	Nayland, Late Seventeenth Century Pargetting, of simple geometrical design, on a cottage at (B.O. *d.*)	47
28.	Suffolk Wrought Iron Casements, now in the Victoria and Albert Museum (See also under London) (B.O. *m.d.*)	74
30. 31.	Suffolk Wrought Iron Casement-fasteners, enlarged details of Fig. 28 (See also under London) (Dorothy M. Buckmaster, *m.d.*)	75
19.	Woolpit, Cottage-roof at (A. H. Powell, *d.*)	40

SURREY

38.	Alfold, Cranleigh, Stile near (A. H. Powell, *d.*)	86
28.	Godalming, Wrought Iron Casement, now in the Victoria and Albert Museum, from (See also under London) (B.O. *m.d.*)	74
29.	Godalming, Enlarged detail of fastener to same (See also under London) (Dorothy M. Buckmaster, *m.d.*)	75
9.	Guildford, A Surrey example of timber-framed construction at (A. H. Powell, *d.*)	29
8.	Guildford, Skeleton of house shown in Fig. 9 (A. H. Powell, *d.*)	28

SUSSEX

11.	A Sussex example of timber-framed construction (A. H. Powell, *d.*)	31
10.	Skeleton of house shown in Fig. 11 (A. H. Powell, *d.*)	30

INDEX TO ILLUSTRATIONS

WARWICKSHIRE

FIG.		PAGE
12.	Kenilworth, South Elevation of Vine Cottage at (E. J. May, *d.*)	36
13.	Kenilworth, West Elevation of Vine Cottage at (E. J. May, *d.*)	37
14.	Kenilworth, Detail at A, Fig. 13, ditto (E. J. May, *d.*)	37
15.	Kenilworth, Detail at B, Fig. 13, ditto (E. J. May, *d.*)	37
16.	Kenilworth, Detail of West Elevation of Central Porch, ditto (See Fig. 12) (E. J. May, *m.d.*)	38
17.	Kenilworth, Details of same (See Figs. 12 and 16) (E. J. May, *m.d.*)	38
18.	Kenilworth, Hinge and other details of door to Porch of same (See Fig. 12) (E. J. May, *m.d.*)	39

WESTMORLAND

| 27. | Townend, Troutbeck, Windermere, Two examples of cylindrical chimneys at (A. H. Powell, *d.*) | 72 |

WILTSHIRE

| 2. | Castle Combe, near Chippenham, Plan of (Ord. Survey) | 12 |

YORKSHIRE

| 7. | Beck Foot, near Bingley, West Riding of Yorks., Detail of Stone Lantern on Kneeler of Gable (B.O. *d.*) | 25 |

Note : *d.* = drawn by.
m.d. = measured drawing by.
B.O. = Basil Oliver.

CALCOT, A COTSWOLD HAMLET, BY THE COLN, ABOVE BIBURY.
GLOUCESTERSHIRE

SYDNEY PITCHER, F.R.P.S.

INTRODUCTION

The Preservation of Old Cottages and the desirability of their retention for those for whom they were built—Old Building Methods and Advice by Contemporary Writers—The Development of the English Cottage—External Charm and lack of Internal Convenience—Landlords—Geological Influences and Local Characteristics—Aerial Photographs and Village Plans—Typical Village, Landscape and Street Views.

THE modern fashion, known as "the week-end habit," is admirable so long as those able to buy old country cottages do not dispossess the poor folk whose dearly-loved homes these are, and for whom they were built. When such buildings are derelict and condemned it is praiseworthy for those in more affluent circumstances to save them from demolition, but nothing is more contemptible than the utterly selfish action of thoughtless town-dwellers who buy up farm-labourers' cottages merely to use them for summer holidays and week-ends, and to leave them empty and unoccupied for the rest of the year, while those turned out are at their wits' end to find homes near their work, or indeed any homes at all.

Even worse is the speculator who does this sort of thing on a large scale and leaves a trail of miserable human victims behind him, and, more often than not, architectural victims as well, for the speculator's idea of restoration and "improvement" is usually of a crude catch-penny order, cheap and shoddy. In the words of architects' specifications he leaves "all perfect on completion," but the charm has vanished.

Rural District Councils are at last alive to the iniquity of these dispossessing practices, and it is gratifying that some have passed resolutions calling for a law to prevent them.

The machinery recently devised by the Ministry of Health for the reconditioning of old cottages is a move in the right direction, but it needs strengthening to coerce those whose function it is to make the Act operable, viz., County Councils. It was Mr. G. K. Chesterton who once reminded us that " rose-covered cottages should not colour our conception too much. The roses are all outside such places ; the thorns are within." There is a great deal of truth in these words, and it is well to bear them in mind in admiring the external picturesqueness of old cottages, or even only the representations of them, but this aspect of the matter is a subject in itself and cannot be more than hinted at in these pages.

One of the disadvantages of living in an old cottage is that the aspect is usually wrong according to modern ideas and knowledge of the health-giving power of sunshine.

It is not by chance that the houses, both large and small of our forefathers face North, for Dr. Andrew Boorde tells us in his *Dyetary of Helth* "the Boke for to lerne a man to be wyse in buylding of his house" (published in 1542) that ". . . the merydyall wynde of all wyndes is the most worste, for the South wynde doth corrupt and doth make euyl vapours. The East wynde is pepōrate, fryske and fragrant, the West wynde is mutable, the North winde purgeth euyll vapoures, wherefor better it is of the two worst yt the wyndowes do open playne North, than playne South. . . ."

This seeming dislike of sunshine prevailed up to Victorian times. One recalls how the old ladies, in Mrs. Gaskell's *Cranford*, protected their new drawing-room carpets with old newspapers, chasing the sunbeams every quarter of an hour.

It is said that even William Morris favoured a North aspect, perhaps because he liked looking out of his windows at the charming effect of sunshine in the garden, without being dazzled, or did he have doubts, one wonders, about the fadeless qualities of his fabrics?

Sir Henry Wotton, writing in 1624, held that the site should be " not subject to any foggy noysomnesse, from Fenns or Marshes neere adjoyning . . . not undigested, for want of Sunne." Thus sun was appreciated, in moderation.

Old cottages were usually built without any foundations, and survive, but Wotton considered that ". . . the Foundation . . . requireth the exactest care. For if that happen to dance it will marre all the mirth of the House. . . ."

He refers to " Doores and Windowes " as " these Inlets of Men and of Light," but he is still more entertaining on the subject of " Staire-cases," thus: ". . . To make a compleate Staircase is a curious peece of Architecture: The vulgar Cautions are these.

" That it have a very liberall Light, against all Casualtie of Slippes, and Falles.

" That the space about the Head, bee large and Airy . . . because a man doth spend much breath in mounting.

" That the Half-paces bee well distributed, at competent distances, for reposing on the way.

" That to avoyd Encounters, and besides to gratifie the beholder, the whole Staire case have no nigard Latitude, that is, for the principall Ascent. . . ."

These are fine ideals but rarely, if ever, adopted for cottages whose builders were more willing to take risks.

The same cautious counseller advocates the making of a " Modell or Type of the whole structure " before commencing to build, and he utters a warning that the said " Modell bee as plaine as may be, without colours or other beautifying lest the pleasure of the Eye preoccupate the

Judgement." These words of wisdom, written before 1624, are just as applicable now.

According to Turner and Parker's *Domestic Architecture of the Middle Ages*, the peasantry, up to the beginning of the fifteenth century, dwelt in one-room huts, built of mud and thatched with reeds or straw. Smoke from the turf fires in these poor and filthy hovels could only find its way out by means of the unglazed window-openings—for at that time there was neither glass nor chimneys—and the discomfort must have been intense.

A labourer's or villein's furniture, usually home-made, consisted of a cupboard, or coffer; a bench; a trestle-table; stools; a few wooden platters; and utensils for cooking, made by the village smith. Later there was a slow and gradual improvement when cottages were increased in size. When this development occurred, and the one-room house gave place to three ground floor rooms, the middle one, by which one entered, was known as the "house-place." The room to the right was the "chamber" in which the family and guests all slept. The smaller room at the opposite end was the larder or "outshott," as it was then called. Occasionally an attic, approached by a ladder, was formed in the roof, for storage purposes.

The Peasant's House, during the second half of the fourteenth century, as described by Piers Plowman,[1] gives some indication of the acute discomfort in which many of the poorer classes lived in those days in the following quotation: ". . . And if his hous be unhiled and reyne on his bedde, He seketh and seketh til he slepe drye. . . ."[2] The floors of these early villein cottages were simply of earth beaten hard by constant use, and so also were they in

[1] Piers Plowman, B. text XVII, 315–326.
[2] i.e. And if his house has a leaky roof, and the rain falls on his bed, he searches and searches till he sleeps dry.

more important buildings such as colleges and churches. Earthen floors were sometimes decorated with animal bones, driven in to a depth of from three to four inches, to form a pattern.

One of the minor inconveniences of life at that time was the periodical digging up of these earthern floors by an individual known as a " saltpetre man."[1] The floors, being porous, absorbed filth in the form of nitrous matters, and it seems that, in this way, the necessary nitre, required in the manufacture of gunpowder, was obtained. These unwelcome visitations had to be tolerated for several centuries and only ceased during the Commonwealth.

Rushes were sometimes strewn on the floors to make the rooms more comfortable and to counteract the dust. Another method, whose place of origin was Italy, was to mix bullock's blood with the mud for the floor, which was thus said to have been given an appearance of black marble, when polished.

Flag-stones, bricks and quarry tiles (called " pamments " in East Anglia) gave a greatly improved finish to the primitive floors, just described, and the use of these materials has been continued up to the present day for the floors of sculleries, larders, lavatories and out-houses, but bedded on concrete instead of being laid on the earth like street pavements.

William Harrison, Rector of Radwinter, in Essex, in the reign of Queen Elizabeth, noted ". . . ye great amendement of lodginge, for sayde they [referring to the oldest inhabitants of his parish in 1577] . . . our fathers and we ourselves have lyen full oft upon straw pallettes covered onely with a sheete under coverlettes made of dagswain or hopharlots (I use their owne termes) and a good round logge under their heades in steade of a boulster. If it were so that our fathers or ye good man of the house had a matteres or flockbed, and thereto a sacke of chafe to rest hys heade upon,

[1] C. F. Innocent: *The Development of English Building Construction*, p. 158.

he thought himself to be well lodged as the Lorde of the towne, so well were they contented. Pillowes sayde they were thought meete onely for women in childebed. As for servants [and presumably the labouring classes generally at that time] if they had any sheete above them, it was well, for seldome had they any under their bodies, to keepe them from the pricking strawes, that ranne oft thorow the canvas, and raced their hardened hides. . . ."

This extract gives us a very clear insight into the life of the common folk and their lack of comforts in Elizabethan times.

England—" the misty island kingdom," as the ex-Kaiser has lately [1] described our land—is famed the world over for the beauty of her villages and cottage-homes. Indeed throughout the British Empire our cousins overseas regard them almost *as* England, when they think of " home." These tiny buildings, often only one room thick, still stand much as they did during the Civil War and in a few cases, but to a lesser extent unchanged, from as far back as the Wars of the Roses.

Undoubtedly they are not the least of the bonds that inspire affection for the Motherland, and sometimes a stimulus to patriotism.

We love them in spite of all their drawbacks—such as absence of indoor sanitation, laid-on water, and so forth— and they are loved, moreover, by those whose families have lived in them for generations, as much as by the mere passer-by.

Their rooms are certainly more spacious and their walls more substantially built than those of modern Council houses. Consequently, together with the fact that they are so frequently thatched, ancient cottages are warmer in

[1] The Ex-Kaiser's Preface to *The Letters of the Empress Frederick*, edited by Sir Frederick Ponsonby.

INTRODUCTION

winter and cooler in summer. Even if their floor-to-ceiling measurement does fall short of the Ministry of Health's eight feet minimum height requirement, and if their windows are not equal to one-tenth of the floor area (to mention only two of many fussy regulations and by-laws), they make, more often than not, extremely cosy and fascinating little homes.

Mr. Alfred Powell—poet as well as architect and painter—has conjured up a delightful vision of ". . . some old cottage planted on a hill-side, set clean and sweet upon the turf . . . its life thenceforth in close touch with the fresh air and fields, the fire daily replenished from the wood near by, the water drawn from the spring or up out of the well. This simple ritual was the background—is still the background—of many a worker's life and health. . . ." [1]

But, unfortunately, it is not all idyllic like that. One must not forget the different types of landlords—good (rare); good, but poor (less rare); poor (common); bad and poor (less common); bad and rich (inexcusable). Our minds instinctively turn back to Mr. Chesterton's roses outside and thorns within.

In former days changes of style were as gradual as natural growth. The late " Jock " Stevenson very succinctly summed up the position in his statement that ". . . when the old styles of architecture flourished . . each age had only one way of working in them ; all others being either inconceivable or false. The only difference consisted in doing better or worse the same things in the same way ; and the changes . . . though obvious when measured over centuries . . . were unnoticed as they occurred. . . ." [2]

These facts particularly apply to rural buildings, remote from fashion and foreign influences, as will presently be

[1] *The Studio Year Book*, 1920, p. 31.
[2] *House Architecture* by J. J. Stevenson, F.R.I.B.A.

observed by an examination of and comparison between the numerous types illustrated in the following pages. In addition the names of many of the villages in which old cottages are situated are often extraordinarily attractive.

By the courtesy of Mr. Sydney R. Jones it is possible to make use of his admirably clear and well drawn Geological Map of England (Fig. 1), which indicates the geological areas into which England is approximately divided, and their yields.

Architecturally by far the most interesting stone-built cottages follow the track of the great oolitic belt, which extends from a little to the north of Brigg in Lincolnshire, southwards through the middle of that county, through Rutland, Northamptonshire, Huntingdonshire and then in a south-westerley direction, covering the north parts of Bedfordshire, Buckinghamshire, Oxfordshire and Berkshire, the south-east of Gloucestershire, southwards again through Wiltshire to the west of Salisbury Plain, east Somerset, south-westwards in Dorset through Sherborne to Crewkerne, and finally south-eastwards down to Portland Bill (No. 3 in Fig. 1). Throughout this area is to be found a highly developed school of building, both for its masonry and timber work.

Towards the west oölitic and liassic limestones are found, and towards the east flint and chalk run parallel with the oölitic belt. This chalk formation extends over the north-west of Norfolk, west Suffolk, north-west Essex, south-east Cambridgeshire, north Hertfordshire, south-east Buckinghamshire, south Oxfordshire, the south of Berkshire —west of Reading—Salisbury Plain in Wiltshire, Hampshire, south-east along the South Downs to Beachy Head, and south-west from Salisbury through Dorset, via Blandford and Dorchester, and then south-east again as far as the locality of Wareham (Nos. 4, 2, 1 in Fig. 1).

Fig. 1.—Geological Map of England.

Drawn by Sydney R. Jones.

The chalk formation, in its north-east part, gives us, in Suffolk, Essex, Cambridgeshire and Hertfordshire, the plasterwork in conjunction with wood construction for which East Anglia is noteworthy.

All the northern counties (Division 5 of Map) comprise another important limestone and sandstone region where roofs are of low pitch and covered with stone slates, larger and heavier than found in the Cotswolds. The buildings are severe in character, as in Cornwall, where the intractable nature of the granite enforces utter simplicity and even a certain grimness.

In parts of Devon and Somerset and in south Wiltshire we have cottages built of "cob" as well as stone, in both cases usually plastered externally and then lime-washed. The repeated coats of lime-wash give a charming texture, not inappropriately of a rich creamy consistency.

Of course the other equally important method of construction is timber-framing with the infilling formed of various materials in a variety of ways. Brickwork, in old work, comes third in importance, and is to be seen at its best in East Anglia, where it is often used in conjunction with flint, more particularly in Norfolk, where foreign influence is more marked than in any other part of England, and where pantiles, as in the east of Yorkshire, are the commonest form of roofing materials.

The timber regions are clearly marked on the map, though the timber-framed cottages of the north-western counties—Lancashire, Cheshire, Staffordshire, Shropshire, Warwickshire, Worcestershire and Herefordshire—have much larger timbers, wider spacing and more elaboration of detail—e.g. the "magpie" work in Cheshire and in the few examples still extant in Lancashire—than in the south-eastern counties of Kent, Surrey and Sussex, as also in Hampshire and in such formerly well-wooded counties as Essex.

ALCONBURY WESTON, HUNTINGDONSHIRE (FROM THE NORTH)
SHOWING THE GREAT NORTH ROAD BY-PASSING THE VILLAGE

Plate 3

WAREHAM, DORSET

PLATE 4

VIEW FROM THE SQUARE, BIBURY, GLOUCESTERSHIRE

COTTAGES NEAR THE UPPER END OF ARLINGTON ROW, BIBURY, GLOUCESTERSHIRE

INTRODUCTION

The aerial view of Alconbury Weston, Huntingdonshire (Plate 2), shows distinctly how the Great North Road by-passes the village, thus affording an examplar for regional planners and road engineers faced with a similar situation.

Another aeroplane photograph, taken from a lower altitude, of Wareham, Dorset (Plate 3) illustrates the *look* of a small country town, of less than two thousand inhabitants; it is typically English both in lay-out and character.

On a smaller scale is Castle Combe, near Chippenham, generally considered to be the prettiest village in Wiltshire, herein represented by two photographic illustrations (Plate 5) and by its plan (Fig. 2), taken from the Ordnance Survey Map. The exceptionally fine Gothic Market Cross is discernible. The little stream of clear water, known as By Brook, greatly adds to the picturesque charm of the village in the same way as does the Windrush at Bourton-on-the-Water and the Coln at Bibury. Their delightful trout streams are the making of these two famous Gloucestershire villages.

By way of contrast a plan (Fig. 3) is given from the east of England, of the little known village of Hartest, where cottages are grouped round a green in a way reminiscent of the better known village of Long Melford in the same locality, though at the latter the houses are on the west side only. The River Glem rises just to the north of Hartest, where it is too diminutive to be of much account.

The Chad Brook, a small tributary of the Stour, crosses under the main road at Melford, but here again this stream does little to enhance the general picturesqueness of the situation owing to it being well to the south of the Green. As a worthy substitute, however, for the water asset we have here the magnificent church and brick almshouses at the top (north) of the Green and that splendid Tudor pile, Melford

Hall, with its park and gardens skirting the main road, on the east side of the Green.

No book has done more to enhance the fame of the Cotswolds—" the grand centre of Elizabethan sport," as its

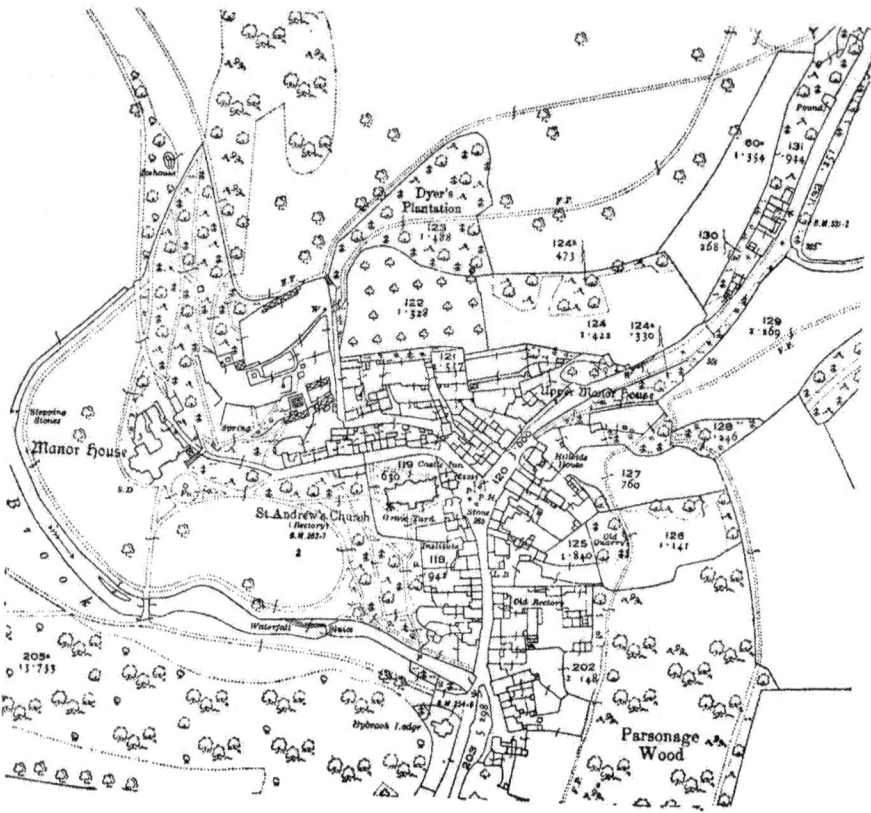

Fig. 2.—Plan of Castle Combe, near Chippenham, Wiltshire (see Plate 5).
(Reproduced from the Ordnance Survey Map with the sanction of the Controller of H.M. Stationery Office.)

author describes it—than J. Arthur Gibbs' delightful account of country life and pursuits in Gloucestershire under the title of *A Cotswold Village*. In this, he writes, with justifiable enthusiasm ". . . Even in winter I do not know any scene more pleasing to the eye than the sight of a Cotswold hamlet nestling amid the stately trees in the valley, if you

Plate 5

CASTLE COMBE, NEAR CHIPPENHAM, WILTSHIRE
VILLAGE STREET, WITH MARKET CROSS
(See Fig. 2)

CASTLE COMBE
VIEW OF VILLAGE FROM TOP OF CHURCH
(See Fig. 2)

Plate 6

CHEDWORTH, SOUTH-WEST OF NORTHLEACH, GLOUCESTERSHIRE

AT CHEDWORTH, GLOUCESTERSHIRE

Plate 7

CHILDS WICKHAM, GLOUCESTERSHIRE, NEAR BROADWAY, WORCESTERSHIRE

OSMOTHERLEY, UNDER THE HAMBLETON HILLS, NEAR NORTHALLERTON, YORKSHIRE

Plate 8

RUNSWICK, NEAR WHITBY, YORKSHIRE

AT SANDSEND, NEAR WHITBY, YORKSHIRE

INTRODUCTION

happen to see it on a fine day. . . ." He delights in the genuineness of the old buildings of " good honest, native stone," and remarks that " the builders may have their faults, their prejudices, and their ignorances—the very

Fig. 3.—Plan of Hartest, near Long Melford, Suffolk.
(Reproduced from the Ordnance Survey Map with the sanction of the Controller of H.M. Stationery Office.)

simplicity may have been the means of saving them from error—but they were at all events truthful and genuine. . . ."

Sheep-farming, in the Cotswold country, had been established in the reign of William the Conqueror, and reached the height of its prosperity in the days of the Tudors. The wealth of those who made their living out of the wool trade is reflected in the fine heritage of building—both ecclesiastical and domestic—still remaining.

In the little villages and hamlets of the Coln Valley, above Fairford and thereabouts, one finds the true Cotswold spirit, even more so than in the better known towns, such as Chipping Campden and Burford, two of the most typical. Calcot (Plate 1), a tiny but unspoiled hamlet, is a quite remarkable survival in these days of rapid change, inappropriate building, needless demolition, apathy, neglect, decay and even a few architectural losses due to transportation.

Bibury (Plate 4) is better known, and deservedly so, for was it not considered, by both William Morris and Arthur Gibbs, to be the loveliest of all English villages?

Chedworth (Plate 6), only a few miles away, possesses the same unaffected charm. Truly this locality is the heart of England. The row of cottages, in the lower of the two illustrations of Chedworth, is of rather later date, but is, however, no less pleasing, although its appeal takes a different form.

Views of Childs Wickham, Gloucestershire, and of Osmotherley, under the Hambleton Hills, near Northallerton, in Yorkshire, each with its village cross, are intentionally illustrated in juxtaposition by way of contrast (Plate 7) to show, at a glance, the intimate and gracious charm of the one and the typical north country burliness of the other. It affords a striking comparison of architectural characters and environments.

The differences in the pitch of the roofs is, in particular, a marked feature in these two illuminating examples from the south-west and north of England.

The same rugged simplicity and low-pitched roofs are apparent again in the east coast Yorkshire villages of Runswick and Sandsend (Plate 8), a little to the north of Whitby.

HIGHAM, NEAR ALFRETON, DERBYSHIRE

BEELEY, NEAR BAKEWELL, DERBYSHIRE

Plate 10

JOHN PEEL'S HOME, AT RUTHWAITE, NEAR CALDBECK, CUMBERLAND

WEARHEAD, NEAR ST. JOHN'S CHAPEL, CO. DURHAM

INTRODUCTION

Both in Derbyshire and in the Moorland district of Staffordshire (adjoining Cheshire and Derbyshire) cottages are of stone with large ashlar door-jambs and window-frames, constructed with big stones, which are bonded into the rubble walls, and often with large quoins—one stone forming a quoin and part of a door-jamb. Window mullions are unmoulded. In both counties gables are seldom carried up above the roof and, as in the south of Staffordshire, blue tiles from the Potteries are to be seen.

Distinctive Derbyshire buildings, at Higham and Beeley are shown on Plate 9. Large stone roofing slates not unlike Horsham slabs, are distinguishable in the foreground of the Beeley group. (See also Plates 37 and 38 of similar roof-coverings in Yorkshire and Dorset, and another Derbyshire example at Eyam on Plate 39.)

Cumberland and County Durham cottages are shown side by side on Plate 10. There is little to be remarked about them except that they are thoroughly representative of their respective counties. All these gable-ended cottages have low-pitched roofs with their ridges running from end to end (and *not* hipped as in the south). At each end of the roof the gable is surmounted by a plain squat chimney. Almost complete absence of eaves-projection tends still further to accentuate their prevailing baldness and austerity.

Cottages in Northumberland are very similar in all respects, as can be seen in Plate 11, but in this delightful picture their stiff angularity makes a good foil to the picturesque pile of Alnwick Castle, with the church on the right, and the prettily wooded landscape in the background.

Three little views of Empingham, Stretton and Barrowden, all near Oakham in our smallest county, serve adequately to typify the cottage-architecture of Rutland (Plate 12). The removal of their original window-casements, and the substitution of single sheets of glass, considerably mars the otherwise satisfactory effect. To what extent may be judged by comparing the two ground floor windows in the middle illustration, and by the striking contrast between the subdivided dormer window lights and the ugly voids below, in the Barrowden house.

This particular fault, which obtains all too generally, just robs the spectator of complete satisfaction, as it will also the reader, in numerous cottages illustrated throughout this book. Fortunately, however, it is a defect that can be remedied in course of time, as public taste reaches a little nearer to the higher standard of educated architectural taste.

Leaving the limestone belt of Rutland and moving in a south-westerly direction through the adjoining county of Leicestershire, and thence through Warwickshire and Worcestershire, we come to the sandstone and timber region adjoining Wales. (See Fig. 1.) The Eardisland timber-built cottages (Plate 13) are typical of Herefordshire and, with the picturesque companion-view of Shaftesbury, Dorset, exhibit the marked dissimilarity between one county and another.

Plate 14 illustrates two more types exemplified by the stone-built and thatched cottages at East Lulworth, in south Dorest, and the fascinating lime-washed and thatched cottages at Bratton, near Minehead, Somerset. Notice the traditional position and form (slightly tapering) of the single side chimney here and in all the best of the old cottages in Somerset, also the rounded projecting (and alas! obsolete) oven of the cottage nearest the camera. Compare the Selworthy cottage (Plate 21) in the same county.

It would be hard to find a more lovely piece of English scenery than the setting of the Devonshire cottages at Salcombe Gullet, in the extreme south of the county, near Kingsbridge (Plate 15).

The views of East Budleigh, Devon, and Godshill, in the Isle of Wight (Plate 16), are purposely put side by side to show

Plate 11

ALNWICK, FROM CLAYPORT, NORTHUMBERLAND

Plate 12

EMPINGHAM, NEAR OAKHAM, RUTLAND

STRETTON, NEAR OAKHAM, RUTLAND

BARROWDEN, NEAR OAKHAM, RUTLAND

Plate 13

AT EARDISLAND, HEREFORDSHIRE
(BETWEEN PEMBRIDGE AND LEOMINSTER)

SHAFTESBURY, DORSET
VIEW LOOKING SOUTH

Plate 14

EAST LULWORTH, NEAR WAREHAM, DORSET

BRATTON, NEAR MINEHEAD, SOMERSET

SALCOMBE GULLET, NEAR KINGSBRIDGE, DEVON

Plate 16

EAST BUDLEIGH, NEAR BUDLEIGH SALTERTON, DEVONSHIRE

GODSHILL, NEAR WROXALL, ISLE OF WIGHT

Plate 17

WHITE NOTLEY, NEAR WITHAM, ESSEX

CHIPPING HILL, WITHAM, ESSEX

Plate 18

KERSEY, NEAR HADLEIGH, SUFFOLK

NEWPORT, ESSEX

Plate 19

AT SENNEN, NEAR LAND'S END, CORNWALL

ANOTHER COTTAGE AT SENNEN, NEAR LAND'S END

Plate 20

OLD POST OFFICE, TINTAGEL, NEAR BOSCASTLE, CORNWALL

Plate 21

AT SELWORTHY, NEAR MINEHEAD, SOMERSET

PLATE 22

AT LUSTLEIGH, NEAR BOVEY TRACEY, DEVON

INTRODUCTION

the *look* of two typical English villages. No town planning, however clever, could have produced such beautiful compositions whose grouping is formed in a perfectly natural manner, conveniently near the parish church, which, in each case, dominates the picture.

In contradistinction to these southern types the timber-framed and plastered cottages of East Anglia (Plates 17 and 18) are interesting. The Suffolk village of Kersey (the upper view on Plate 18 and Fig. 4) is second to none in the Eastern Counties, and is one of the prettiest villages in England. That it has been so little spoilt is probably due to its secluded position, tucked in a little valley, away from main roads.

Fig. 4.—Kersey, Suffolk, from the North.

CHAPTER I

STONE-BUILT COTTAGES

Poor foundations of early types—Cornish granite-building—Traditional position of chimney in Somerset—Admixture of flint in bands and chequerwise in Wiltshire and Dorset—Cotswold Types—Examples of Devon, Somerset, Dorset, Wilts., Glos., Worcs., Berks., Oxon, Yorks, Derbyshire, Northumberland, Leicestershire and Northants Cottages.

In cottage building undressed stone, often of great size, was used only as foundation and plinth for a wooden-framed superstructure, with wattle and clay filling, before it was used more extensively for the whole walling. The stones then used were only those that could be easily gathered from the surface of the land, from river beds or from boulder clay.

For the more humble buildings it was not until the Renaissance that worked stone or "ashlar" began to be used generally.[1]

Settlements were sometimes caused by these rough and fragmentary foundations through the absence of mortar with its cohesive quality.

Probably these not unnatural foundational troubles and recurring collapses of mediæval stone buildings caused mistrust and led the builders of those days to pin their faith more to carpenters than to masons. A striking instance of this lack of confidence in stone was the case of a large barn at Peterborough (now destroyed) where the entire roof was carried by timber supports quite independent of the outer

[1] C. F. Innocent, *The Development of English Building Construction*, p. 118.

stone walls, which were a mere casing. When these were removed the great roof still stood intact.[1]

Commencing the subject of stone-built cottages with the extreme West of England it should be mentioned that until recently " clem " or " cob " (dialect names for mud walls) was used equally in Cornwall with the rough granites of that county, but it is difficult to date granite owing to its impervious nature and lack of detail by reason of its hardness.

" . . . The humble Cornish builder of ancient and modern times set in huge masses of granite just as he found them, and the larger they were the better they answered his purpose ; if he could make three or four great blocks of stone form a wall, the less labour and skill was required in building, and the main object was obtained. . . ."[2]

Relative to this fact the late Mr. C. F. Innocent, in his excellent book, observes " . . . This agrees with the rule that the fewer the joints the more primitive is the construction, and is not entirely due to a wish to save labour, although methods of building are always conditioned to some extent by the materials. . . ."[3]

Examples of the use of such massive blocks of granite are shown on Plate 19 of two cottages at Sennen, near Land's End. In these the limitations of the material are clearly seen. Their masculine and rugged character is very befitting to their exposed position. Note the rough-hewn shaped granite door-head in the lower illustration. The block of granite known as the Tablêmen, in front of the upper cottage, is of some historic interest, and has probably given the name to the estate on which it stands. Main or Mên is Cornish for Stone. According to tradition this block of granite, 7 ft. 10 in. long by 3 ft. high, is said to have

[1] *Annual Report of the Society for the Protection of Ancient Buildings*, 1892.
[2] J. T. Blight, *Churches of West Cornwall*, p. 166.
[3] *The Development of English Building Construction*, pp. 119, 120.

STONE-BUILT COTTAGES

served as a dining-table for seven Saxon Kings who are reputed to have foregathered at that remote spot in solemn conclave.

Plate 20 illustrates the better known Old Post Office at Tintagel, a building which happily has been acquired, in recent years, by the National Trust, and put in good repair. The haphazard form and growth of this picturesque group has undoubted charm, and nothing could better express the locality. It could only have been built in Cornwall.

Plate 22, of Lustleigh, near Bovey Tracey, Devon, and Plate 23, of Allerford, near Porlock, Somerset, form two extremely beautiful compositions quite out of the common. The last-named rather reminds one of a successful piece of work by an imaginative scenic-artist, yet it actually exists in this wonderful country of ours.

Somerset cottages, and many in Devonshire also, originally had only one fireplace, with external projection, and that at the side of the house often adjacent to the entrance.

The cottage at Selworthy, near Minehead, Somerset (Plate 21), well illustrates this traditional arrangement and incidentally it possesses, to a marked degree, the elusive quality of homely charm, and is quite irresistible.

Additional chimneys, built subsequently, are easily recognisable, in many instances, by their meanness.

The two Dorset cottages, one at Melbury Abbas, near Shaftesbury, and the other at Bridport which appear together (Plate 24) have all the fascination of numberless unpretentious thatched dwelling, to be found scattered all about the Wessex country. Note how greatly the character of each is attributable to the form and size of windows.

Compare very similar cottages at East Lulworth and Morden, both near Wareham, in the same county (Plates 71 and 86).

The effectiveness of horizontal bands or of chequer-patterns formed of alternating stone and flints can be studied from the splendid examples of these treatments illustrated on Plates 25 and 26. The striped house at Puddletown, near Dorchester, is less usual in Dorset than the chequer-work (here used somewhat tentatively) shown in the singularly beautiful view of Fisherton-de-la Mere, in the Wylye Valley of Wiltshire (to the north-west of Salisbury). In that district there is a whole group of villages—all with unusual and delightful names—where flint, stone and brick are successfully used in conjunction, but these villages and the method of building adopted in them are further referred to in Chapter V.

Sad to relate the roof has fallen in since the photograph was taken of the fine group of stone cottages at Nunney, Somerset (Plate 27). The whole row, dating probably from the last quarter of the sixteenth century, is now in a deplorable state of dilapidation. Nunney Castle, seen in the distance, was going the same way until its rescue by H.M. Office of Works. It is to be hoped that in due course, before it is too late, this neglected property will come into more appreciative ownership, and the walls of the cottages be saved from complete collapse. Obviously the pantiled upper part of the roof is repair work and not as old as the stone-slated gables, which are akin to those on Arlington Row, Bibury, Gloucestershire (Plates 28 and 29). The latter, in turn, is strongly reminiscent of the pleasant Wiltshire group from Hudswell (lower illustration on Plate 27). The Bibury and Nunney gables are much alike, but at Hudswell it will be observed that the gables are set higher above the main eaves and that most of the windows have labels, or weather-mouldings, over them.

The unique group of cottages, known as Arlington Row, Bibury, Gloucestershire (Plates 28 and 29, and see also Plate 4), a very fine type of perfect Cotswold building, has lately come into prominence through the Royal Society of Arts' appeal for funds for its purchase and reparation.

The appreciative owner, in his keen anxiety that these cottages should not be spoiled, offered to hand them over for a small figure, to the Royal Society of Arts, on condition that they should be put into a proper state of repair. The first part of the transaction is now an accomplished fact and as soon as a sufficient sum has been collected, the reparation (now proceeding) of these eight cottages will be completed, after which the property will be transferred to the care of local trustees, and thus they will be saved for the nation. This is only one instance of the value of the R.S.A. Cottage Preservation Fund, which deserves every encouragement and continuous financial support for the admirable work it is doing.

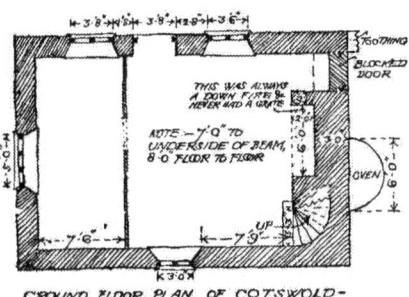

Fig. 5.

There is a sense of peaceful calm as well as a complete lack of self-consciousness about the thatched groups of cottages on Ebrington Hill, near Chipping Campden (Plate 30). Luckily there is no car in sight to spoil the serenity of Mr. Pitcher's charming picture.

Another Cotswold manner—inclusive of chimneys, gables, stone-slates and other local features—is shown in two more attractive groups (Plate 31) at Sevenhampton and Stanton, both in Gloucestershire.

Figs. 5 and 6 illustrate, by plan and perspective sketch, a very modest two-room cottage (demolished in 1919), formerly standing at Tunley, near Sapperton, in the same county. It is far too primitive for modern standards of living and serves to show that we have little or nothing to learn from the planning of old cottages.

Plates 32, 33, 34, 35 and 36, of Western and South-Western types, exhibit most attractive diversity of design, chiefly in the combination of stone walling with thatched roofs, but it is a melancholy reflection that drawing-board and tee-square architecture rarely achieves such engaging results.

Fig. 6—Cottage at Tunley. (For plan see Fig. 5.)

Though now cottages, the picturesque group at Beck Foot, near Bingley, West Riding of Yorkshire, has a history. Dated 1617 (over a doorway), the property formerly belonged to the Knights of St. John of Jerusalem, whose symbol of ownership is indicated by the stone lanterns of the gable (Plate 37 and Fig. 7), a very interesting and unusual feature.

The cottages at Kilburn, near Thirsk, Yorkshire (Plate 38), supply an instance of the very gradual and tentative use of stone, for here in the nearest cottage, only the ground floor walls are of stone with the upper floor timber-framed.

With the destruction of forests in the seventeenth century the price of timber increased and so it came about that it was as cheap to use stone.

The other subject, on the same plate, from Sutcliffe Wood, Shibden Dale, near Halifax, is the more normal York-

AT ALLERFORD, NEAR PORLOCK, SOMERSET

Plate 24

AT MELBURY ABBAS, NEAR SHAFTESBURY, DORSET

AT BRIDPORT, DORSET

Plate 25

AT PUDDLETOWN, NEAR DORCHESTER, DORSET

Plate 26

FISHERTON-DE-LA-MERE, NEAR WYLYE, WILTSHIRE

Plate 27

AT NUNNEY, NEAR FROME, SOMERSET
SHOWING THE CASTLE IN BACKGROUND

AT HUDSWELL, CORSHAM, NEAR CHIPPENHAM, WILTSHIRE

PLATE 28

ARLINGTON ROW, BIBURY, NEAR FAIRFORD, GLOUCESTERSHIRE

SYDNEY PITCHER, F.R.P.S.

Plate 29

ARLINGTON ROW, BIBURY, NEAR FAIRFORD, GLOUCESTERSHIRE
(A NEAR VIEW)

Photo. Sidney Pickess, F.R.P.S.

Plate 30

AT TOP OF EBRINGTON HILL, NEAR CHIPPING CAMPDEN, GLOUCESTERSHIRE

Plate 31

STANTON, GLOUCESTERSHIRE
(BETWEEN WINCHCOMBE AND BROADWAY)

AT SEVENHAMPTON, NEAR CHELTENHAM, GLOUCESTERSHIRE

Plate 32

AT STUDLAND, NEAR SWANAGE, DORSET

AT WOOLSTONE, NEAR FARINGDON, BERKSHIRE

PLATE 33

AT BROADWAY, WORCESTERSHIRE

Plate 34

FINSTOCK POST OFFICE, NEAR CHARLBURY, OXFORDSHIRE

AT DINDER, NEAR WELLS, SOMERSET

Plate 35

AT GREAT TEW, NEAR CHIPPING NORTON, OXFORDSHIRE

AT GREAT TEW, NEAR CHIPPING NORTON, OXFORDSHIRE

Plate 36

AT WESTFORD, NEAR WELLINGTON, SOMERSET

AT YEALMPTON, NEAR PLYMOUTH, DEVONSHIRE

Plate 37

AT SWANAGE, DORSET

AT BECK FOOT, NEAR BINGLEY, WEST RIDING OF YORKSHIRE
(See Fig. 7)

Plate 38

KILBURN, NEAR THIRSK, YORKSHIRE

AT SUTCLIFFE WOOD, SHIBDEN DALE, NEAR HALIFAX, YORKSHIRE

Plate 39

AT EYAM, NEAR TIDESWELL, DERBYSHIRE

AT WEST BOAT, NEAR HEXHAM, NORTHUMBERLAND

STONE-BUILT COTTAGES

shire type entirely in stone, as can also be seen by reference to Plates 7, 8 and 37.

Plate 39, the ominously named Plague Cottages, at Eyam (pronounced Eem), near Tideswell, Derbyshire, serve to perpetuate a terrible year in the annals of this village, for in 1665 —the year of the Great Plague of London— no less than 267 of its inhabitants died of plague, out of a population of 350. Heroic efforts were made by the rector, the Rev. William Mompesson, when the village was isolated, and he was assisted by the then Earl of Devonshire who supplied provisions from outside. These and other necessities

AT BECK FOOT, NEAR BINGLEY, WEST RIDING OF YORKSHIRE, DETAIL OF STONE LANTERN ON KNEELER OF GABLE

Fig. 7. (See also Plate 37.)

were paid for with money placed in troughs of running water. For over a year the rector and his wife, with the aid of the Rev. Thomas Stanley, a former rector who still resided in the village, nobly devoted themselves to the sick and dying, but in August, 1666, when there was a renewed outbreak, Mrs. Mompesson herself fell a victim to the scourge as well as most of the survivors of the earlier outbreak. The infection was said to have been spread, from clothing sent to Eyam from a London tailor's.

It is perhaps worthy of note that the wooden lights of the windows in these Eyam cottages slide horizontally, as often found in Yorkshire, one in front of the other, and are not hinged to open outwards.

The lower example on the same plate is from West Boat, near Hexham, Northumberland. Though rather plain and bald it is a good Northumbrian type.

In the east of Leicestershire—a county, for the most part, of ugly villages full of commonplace nineteenth century cottages—there are a few old cottages and farmhouses built of the beautiful oolitic limestone which is quarried in the adjoining county of Rutland, at Ketton and other well known quarries. These are roofed with Colley Weston slates, or with thatch as at Hallaton (Plate 40).

In the vicinity of Charnwood Forest (so called) the native stone, of a granite-like nature, was used to a considerable extent, the roofs were covered with Swithland slates, but these slate quarries have not, alas! been worked for many years.

The companion subject is from Wicken, a Northamptonshire village, but in the same district. The chief point of interest in this pleasant group is the recessing of the dormer-windows in the thatched roof. Where the channellings in the thatch occur the roof is tiled. From inside the attic bedrooms the light as well as the view must necessarily be restricted. This recessed arrangement gives rather the effect of blinkers and has a decided disadvantage for the inhabitants though ease of construction and a certain external picturesque quality must be conceded.

Plate 40

AT WICKEN, NORTHAMPTONSHIRE

AT HALLATON, SOUTH-EAST LEICESTERSHIRE

Plate 41

AT ALLOSTOCK, LOWER PEOVER, NEAR KNUTSFORD, CHESHIRE

SWIRRES EYE, NEAR WILMSLOW, EAST CHESHIRE

CHAPTER II

TIMBER-FRAMED COTTAGES WITH STUDDING EXPOSED

The various Types and Regional Characteristics—Skill and Knowledge of the Old Carpenters—Methods of In-filling and Finishing—Representative Examples from different parts of England.

TIMBER-YIELDING districts of Mediæval times are indicated on the Geological Map (Fig. 1). In the North there were timber-framed buildings in the east of Yorkshire and Lincolnshire ; in the west and south of Lancashire ; and in the west midlands group of counties, consisting of Cheshire, Staffordshire, Shropshire, Warwickshire, Worcestershire and Herefordshire.

In East Anglia and the counties nearer London on its east, north and west sides were situated the forests—particularly in Essex—whence came most of the ship-building timber.

The South-Eastern group of counties, to the south of the Thames, comprising Kent, Surrey, Sussex, and Hampshire was the third great indigenous forest area. The Weald of Kent and Sussex which was, before the days of coal, the centre of the iron-smelting industry, was so denuded of timber for that purpose—as well as for that of ship-building which took the best of the timber available—that there was an actual shortage of heavy timber required for house construction. These facts are visibly reflected in the characteristics of the several groups to which reference has been made.

In the first-mentioned district, more remote from the depleting influences of other requirements, timber was used in larger sizes, and without stint, and sometimes extravagantly, but where it had to be used more sparingly smaller sizes, with greater refinement of mouldings and carving, are evident.

Fig. 8.

The inaccessibility of this area tended to conserve its timber and to preserve its native character uninfluenced by foreign fashions and craftsmen.

Thus the West may be said to be more purely English, but whether or not this is thought to be a virtue rather depends upon where one was born.

Mr. Alfred H. Powell's drawings (Figs. 8, 9, 10 and 11) show, in a delightful manner the " . . . choice and shaping

PLATE 42

AT ABBOTS BROMLEY, EAST OF STAFFORD

AT VOWCHURCH, IN THE GOLDEN VALLEY, HEREFORDSHIRE

PLATE 43

AT PEMBRIDGE, NEAR LEOMINSTER, HEREFORDSHIRE

ALSO AT PEMBRIDGE, HEREFORDSHIRE

TIMBER-FRAMED COTTAGES

of timber to make it do as much as possible, and with a pleasant sense of strength in the use of it. . . . The illustrations of oak framing, in skeleton and as completed, from Sussex and Surrey, are," he writes, " intended to show what

Fig. 9—A Surrey example of timber-framed construction, at Guildford.

a dramatic work it was putting together these great timbers of our domestic cage." He mentions that the angle posts " are called teasle posts. They are cut from the bole of the tree and used inverted, root end upwards in order to give room for the double corner joint."[1]

[1] *Country Building and Handicraft in Ancient Cottages and Farmhouses:* The Studio Year Book, 1920, pp. 33 and 34.

Another illuminating reason for this practice is referred to by Mr. C. F. Innocent who explains, " that this was for the purpose of allowing the sap to run out by the same way as it had entered the timber, but it is uncertain," he says, " whether this is traditional."[1] Elsewhere in his book he quotes the case of a wooden fence, then seventy-four years

Fig. 10.

old where ". . . it was found that all the parts which were fixed in the same direction as the growth of the timber had rotted, but that those which were inverted had remained sound. . . ."[2]

Mr. Powell, in reference to his illustrations of skeleton framing, especially draws attention to the joinery. ". . .

[1] *The Development of English Building Construction*, p. 165.
[2] Ibid, p. 75, quoted from *The Builder*, XII (1854), p. 468.

Plate 44

AT STONELEIGH, NEAR KENILWORTH, WARWICKSHIRE

AT HOPTON CASTLE, SOUTH-WEST SHROPSHIRE

Plate 45

THE SMITHY, DUNCHURCH, NEAR RUGBY, WARWICKSHIRE

WIXFORD, NEAR ALCESTER, WARWICKSHIRE

TIMBER-FRAMED COTTAGES

When it was first invented cannot be told," he says, " but the mortise and tenon must have been in use from the beginnings of history. All our framed oak buildings and furniture depended upon it for their strength, and the strain sometimes put upon this joint has been enough to rend the upright post rather than affect the joint. It is an interesting

Fig. 11.—A Sussex example of timber-framed construction.

example, if a simple one, of the mastery belonging to all true craftsmanship. . . ."[1]

After the low dwarf wall of stone, brick or flintwork, to form a plinth, had been built, usually direct upon the turf without anything in the nature of a damp-proof course, a substantial oak sill was laid to form a base. Into this vertical

[1] *Country Building and Handicraft in Ancient Cottages and Farmhouses* : The Studio Year Book, 1920, pp. 33 and 34.

posts were tenoned, the larger ones, already referred to, being fixed at the four or more corners of the building. These supported horizontal head-pieces just below the level of the upper floor the walls of which were sometimes flush with those of the ground floor (as in Figs. 10 and 11 of a Sussex house), or else they projected at back and front (as in Figs. 8 and 9 illustrating an old cottage in High Street, Guildford, both without and with the panels, formed by the timber-framing, filled in).

Very often in the fifteenth or early sixteenth century houses were built with their upper storey projecting on three or all four sides. In such cases ". . . which were common in the south-east of England, but rare in the north, a large beam was run diagonally across the building, and into this the joists of the upper floor were framed : the joists on each side of the beam were at right angles to each other. This beam is called a dragon beam, and it has been assumed that this is an ignorant corruption of diagonal beam ; more probably it is the beam upon which the joists seem to draw or pull. . . . The ends of the dragon beam were carried by an angle or corner post, which was fixed with the projection either to the interior, or to the exterior ; in the latter case it was visible from the outside, and was often carved. . . ."[1]

The reason for the projecting upper storey is not quite clear. In narrow streets it is said to be for the purpose of gaining space without encroaching on the footway below. But this theory does not explain the reason for the same practice where there is no such restriction of space, for example in an isolated country house (as in Plate 46). It is more probable that this manner of building was felt to afford some protection to the outer walls of the ground floor. It did at least provide a good " drip " and, in that way, more than halved the amount of water streaming down

[1] *The Development of English Building Construction*, pp. 164 and 165.

Plate 46

AT LOWER TUFFLEY, NEAR GLOUCESTER

AT NORTON, NEAR WORCESTER

Plate 47

AT TROTSHILL, NEAR WORCESTER

AT LITTLE COMBERTON, NEAR PERSHORE, WORCESTERSHIRE

the face of the building. Mr. Innocent opines that it was a survival from the overhanging top defensive galleries of fortified castles.

The whole of the oak-framed cage was tenoned and pinned together. Large oak ceiling-beams, often elaborately carved and moulded, occur at intervals and these support the lesser joists, notched to them, whose size and span is proportionately reduced (see Fig. 10). The walls of the upper storey are similarly constructed, the head forming the roof plate to take the feet of the rafters which are notched on their undersides on to the plate.

Braces and other necessary structural features are shown in all four drawings, and it will be noticed that the close spacing of the lesser vertical studs in the Sussex house is somewhat similar to the East Anglian tradition (as in Plate 56), whilst wide spacing of large timbers only in the Surrey cottage is not unlike the half-timber work of the West (compare various examples).

The panels between the timbers of the oak cage were filled in with a variety of materials in a good many different ways. Perhaps the most general was a kind of lattice of intertwining hazel sticks—rather like a wattle hurdle. This screen was daubed from both sides with clay mixed with chopped straw, hence its description " wattle and daub," (or dab).

The liability of shrinkage of this clay mortar led, chiefly in the seventeenth and eighteenth centuries, to external plastering to keep out the draughts and, for the same reason; also to the use of lime plastering internally, just as the rich man's equivalent way of making his house more comfortable (and incidentally more beautiful) was by means of tapestry and oak-panelling.

In rare cases grooves were cut in the sides of studs to overcome this trouble.

An infilling of brick or "brick-nogging," as it is called, began to be used where and when the revival of brick making made bricks conveniently obtainable. In herring-bone brick filling, which is so much admired, the bricks were laid diagonally for the very practical reason of keeping the vertical joints tight by gravitation.

In the south-western counties (e.g., Wiltshire and Dorsetshire) alternate layers of flint and brick were used for the infilling, and there is a charming old unrestored house at Bignor, in Sussex, with flints alone used for that purpose, in one part of the front, but this is exceptional.

The oak-framed thatched roof type of Wealden cottage usually had its walls wattled with osiers and plastered with a mixture of clay and chopped straw as in East Anglia, Berkshire and generally in the lowlands of England, as in the lowlands abroad, where it was very common.

Post and truss buildings, of the fifteenth, sixteenth and seventeenth centuries, remain in large numbers all over the country, this kind of construction reached its zenith during the reigns of the Tudor sovereigns, and wherever the necessary timber was plentiful there the surviving examples remain more numerous.

In the sixteenth century horizontal timbers began to be more extensively used. When combined with vertical studs panels were formed. These became larger as timber became scarcer, and thus developed the type of work known as "post and pan" (pan meaning pane or panel).

The upper half of Plate 41 well exemplifies this economical development, although in this Cheshire cottage at Allostock the panels are brick-nogged (lime-washed), which probably means that either it is late work or that bricks have been substituted for the original plaster panels "... filled in with a basket work osier foundation, daubed over with clay strengthened with stringy weeds. The finish-

Plate 48

AT FLEET, NEAR FARNBOROUGH, HAMPSHIRE

AT POTTERNE, DEVIZES, WILTSHIRE

Plate 49

AT SUTTON COURTNEY, ABINGDON, BERKSHIRE

AT FRAMPTON-ON-SEVERN, NEAR STROUD, GLOUCESTERSHIRE

ing coat is of plaster on both sides, richly matted with hair, and frequently set back half an inch or more. . . ."[1]

The larger size of timbers, the coarseness and simplicity of detail in their moulded parts, and the primitiveness of carving, if any, in the North and West of England, in comparison with the Eastern and South-Eastern Counties, have already been referred to in the Introduction.

The lower subject, curiously named Swirres Eye, near Wilmslow, in East Cheshire, plainly shows the massiveness of the timbering but hardly an economy in its use.

The so-called " magpie " work is supposed to be decorative but when it is tricked up with superfluous preservatives by misguided restorers it becomes too staring and altogether tiresome. The best point about this building is the fine roof covering of large thick stone slates.

There is an almost feminine daintiness (admittedly emphasised by the effect of snow) about the upper cottage, but the very opposite quality in the one below it. Both would be equally likeable if only the strong " bones " of the more masculine cottage could be " de-creosoted."

Plates 42 and 43 illustrate more of this Western timber building, three of the examples being in Herefordshire and one in Staffordshire, at Abbots Bromley. In South Staffordshire half-timber walls, with thatched roofs, are the chief characteristics of old cottages, and the larger houses seem to have been tiled with blue tiles from the Potteries. " . . . The modern blue Staffordshire ridge tiles without flanges are evidently copies of the old stone ridges. The stone slated roofs of Yorkshire were rarely hipped, but sometimes they were and the angle was then covered with stones similar to the ridges. . . ."[2] The ridge tiles of these Abbots Bromley cottages are, however, flanged, as can be seen.

[1] *Old Halls of Lancashire and Cheshire.*
[2] C. F. Innocent: *The Development of English Building Construction*, p. 183.

Vine Cottage, Kenilworth, Warwickshire, (Figs. 12, 13, 14, 15, 16, 17 and 18), illustrated by sketch-elevations and measured details, made many years ago by Mr. E. J. May, F.R.I.B.A., is a very delightful little building, apparently of Jacobean date judging by the character of the porch details (Figs. 16 and 17). The stone base and timber framing, all pegged together, are carefully recorded. This subject well

Fig. 12.—Vine Cottage, Kenilworth, Warwickshire, South Elevation.

illustrates the method of construction already described and it is interesting to compare this Warwickshire cottage with the framing of the Surrey and Sussex examples (Figs. 8, 9, 10 and 11). Vine Cottage seems to be somewhat later in date than the southern ones which are rather more substantial. The close spacing of the ground floor vertical studs is unusual in the Midlands The infilling of bricks laid horizontally, instead of herring-bone fashion in these narrow spaces, will also be noticed.

TIMBER-FRAMED COTTAGES

Other Warwickshire cottages at Stoneleigh, near Kenilworth (Plate 44); those at Dunchurch, near Rugby, and at Wixford, near Alcester (Plate 45) bear close regional resemblances, but the loving care and thought displayed in all the details of Vine Cottage (Figs. 16, 17 and 18), clearly denote a certain superiority and greater costliness in building, though there is little to choose in charm between the Kenil-

Fig. 13.—Vine Cottage, Kenilworth, West Elevation.

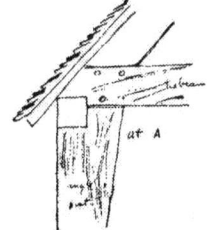

Fig. 14.—Vine Cottage, Kenilworth (see A, Fig. 13).

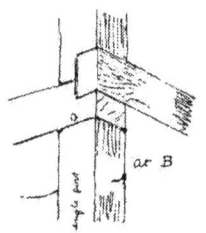

Fig. 15.—Vine Cottage, Kenilworth (see B, Fig. 13).

worth and Stoneleigh examples. Both are thoroughly characteristic of the rural architecture of the county, at its best.

The picturesque group (also on Plate 44) from Hopton Castle, in South-West Shropshire, is so placed for comparative purposes, but at a distinctly humbler level than that of Vine Cottage, Kenilworth.

Plates 46 to 51, and Plate 53, illustrate numerous examples of the widely-spaced timber construction already described.

These are from Gloucestershire, Worcestershire, Hants., Wilts., Berks., Bucks., and Oxon. The herring-bone brick nogging in the "post and pan" cottages at Fleet, Hamp-

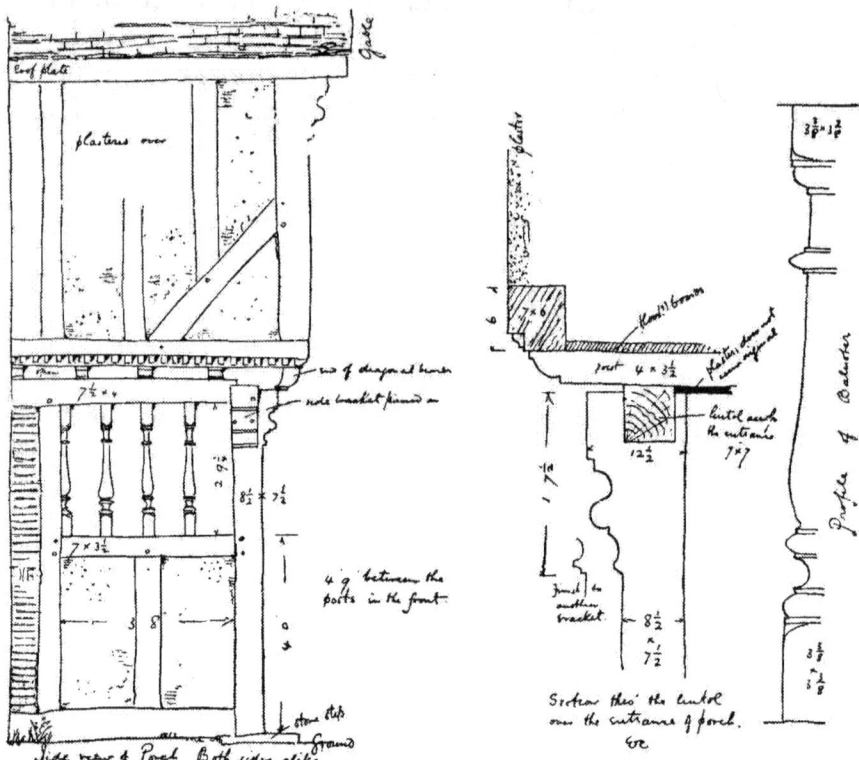

Fig. 16.—Vine Cottage, Kenilworth: Detail of West Elevation of Central Porch (see South Elevation, Fig. 12).

Fig. 17.—Vine Cottage, Kenilworth: Details of Porch (see Figs, 12 and 13).

shire (Plate 48) is not often found in this type and it therefore makes a welcome variant.

The diversity and beauty of much of the village architecture of Steventon, near Abingdon, Berkshire, is noteworthy. (See Plates 50, 51 and 94). Here undoubtedly is a case for national preservation. Amongst other villages that come in this category are Bibury, Gloucestershire; Castle Combe,

Plate 50

KETTLEBROOK, STEEP, NEAR PETERSFIELD, HAMPSHIRE

STEVENTON, NEAR ABINGDON, BERKSHIRE, dated 1657
(See also Plates 51 and 94)

Plate 51

AT STEVENTON, NEAR ABINGDON, BERKSHIRE
(See also Plates 50 and 94)

AT THAME, OXFORDSHIRE

and Lacock, both near Chippenham, Wiltshire; Kersey and Lavenham, Suffolk; Finchingfield, Essex; Pembridge, Herefordshire, and Chiddingstone, Kent, to name only a few. It is interesting to know for certain that the picturesque Steventon group was built during the Commonwealth, and a year before the death of Oliver Cromwell, in 1658.

Newtown Linford is one of the more attractive villages in Leicestershire. A cottage there is shown on Plate 52, but

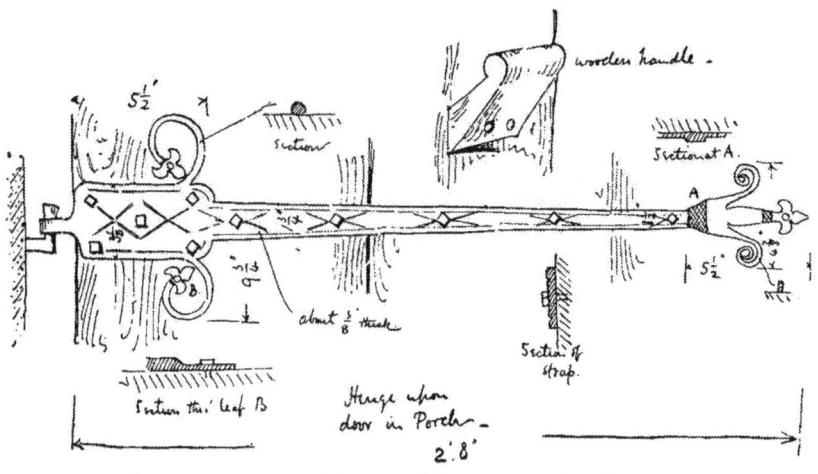

Fig. 18.—Vine Cottage, Kenilworth: Hinge and other details of door to Porch (see Fig. 12).

its companion subject of another at Aldbury, near Tring, Hertfordshire, is one of those diminishing rarities an English village with its old stocks still *in situ*.

Three Nottinghamshire cottages make up Plate 54. That at Normanton-on-Soar, with its closely spaced vertical studs, is more like East Anglian timber-work, except for the small raking struts or braces to the inadequate angle-posts. Herring-bone brick-nogging, or infilling, (as at Fleet, Hants.), is again discernible in the left-hand gable from Sutton Bonington, but the middle subject, from the same village, has the greatest interest though little beauty withal.

It merely happens to be important because there is only one other example in this book (see also gable-end of Newton Linford cottage, Plate 52), of the efficient, but ugly, cruck construction, i.e., formed of curved tree principals reaching to the floor which method is described at being built " on crucks." These are in fact curved props. There are many such in the district about Sheffield and they are also to be found elsewhere in the North of England, the Midlands and in North Wales. The more architecturally sensitive natives of the South-Eastern group of counties would never have tolerated so unsightly a form of construction.

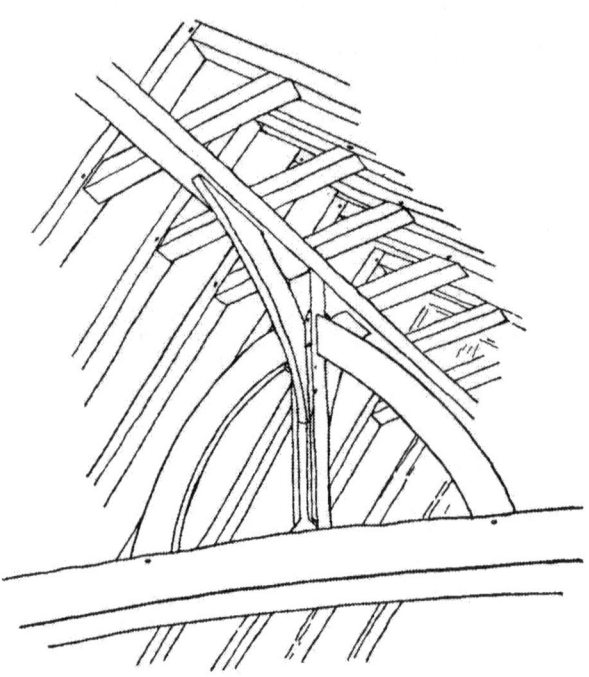

Fig. 19.—Cottage-roof, at Woolpit, Suffolk (between Bury St. Edmunds and Stowmarket).

Bedfordshire is not rich in old cottages, at least of any great merit, but one thought worthy of inclusion herein, for its picturesque quality, is to be found at Ravensden, near Bedford (Plate 55). Its more attractive companion, on the same plate, is yet another jolly group from the famous Herefordshire village of Pembridge, near Leominster.

The last two half-plates of this section are East Anglian, both being of Lavenham, Suffolk (Plate 56). They show very

PLATE 52

AT ALDBURY, NEAR TRING, HERTFORDSHIRE

AT NEWTON LINFORD, NORTH-WEST OF LEICESTER

Plate 53

AT SIMPSON, NEAR FENNY STRATFORD, BUCKINGHAMSHIRE

AT EAST CLAYDON, BETWEEN BUCKINGHAM AND AYLESBURY, BUCKINGHAMSHIRE

Plate 54

AT NORMANTON-ON-SOAR,
SOUTH NOTTINGHAMSHIRE
(NEAR LOUGHBOROUGH, LEICS.)

AT SUTTON BONINGTON,
SOUTH NOTTINGHAMSHIRE
(SHOWING CRUCKS)

AT SUTTON BONINGTON,
SOUTH NOTTINGHAMSHIRE
(NEAR LOUGHBOROUGH, LEICS.)

Plate 55

AT PEMBRIDGE, NEAR LEOMINSTER, HEREFORDSHIRE

AT RAVENSDEN, NEAR BEDFORD

Plate 56

LADY STREET, LAVENHAM, SUFFOLK
(LOOKING TOWARDS WATER STREET)

WATER STREET, LAVENHAM, SUFFOLK
(AT JUNCTION WITH LADY STREET)
Note the mediaeval shop-front, discovered a few years ago

markedly their divergence from the Western types. The buildings illustrated are earlier in date and are probably of the late fifteenth century. The mediæval shop-front (seen in both views) must be of its kind, almost unique. It was, until a few years ago, entirely hidden by plaster which being removed revealed an unsuspected treasure. Only the middle of the three Tudor-headed openings has been reglazed, the side openings remaining blocked (it no longer being a shop). Note the delicate little shaftings on some of the lower studs, and the chamfered brackets springing from them. These details are very typical of this part of England.

The roof of a tiny Suffolk cottage at Woolpit (only nine miles from Lavenham as the crow flies) illustrates (Fig. 19), a fully developed piece of carpentry. With its shortened post carried, with its load, on to a cross beam and so on to the walls, it was possibly to supersede the old king-post which originally reached to the floor in the earlier form of construction. The grace and refinement of the struts are remarkable for so humble a dwelling. How different is the workmanship in a house of this class nowadays!

CHAPTER III

TIMBER-FRAMED, CLAY-LUMP, COB AND STONE COTTAGES, PLASTERED EXTERNALLY

Composition of old plaster—Ornamental Pargetting—Essex "Stickwork," Pricked and Combed Patterns—Clay Lump—Cob and Stone with plain Whitewashed Surfaces—Examples.

A GREAT number—probably the great majority—of the old cottages in this country are plastered externally. Those of timber-framed construction, with wattle and daub filling between the timbers, are very numerous in the Home Counties, East Anglia and the South-East of England. In most cases they were plastered externally at the time they were built, while in others a protective coat of plaster was applied a century or two later, as, for example, the well known fifteenth-century cottage adjoining the churchyard at Clare, Suffolk, which was covered with ornamental pargetting in the seventeenth century. Such an elaborate treatment, in bold relief, is rare on humble cottages but was reserved for rather more important buildings like Sparrow's House (now vaguely called The Ancient House) at Ipswich; Colneford House, at Earl's Colne, Essex; The Limes, Prittlewell, Essex (now demolished); the old River Police Barracks, at Wivenhoe, Essex; the former Sun Inn, at Saffron Walden, and Crown House, Newport, both in Essex, to mention only some of the better known East Anglian examples.

One finds less ambitious and more fragmentary uses of

PLATE 57

AT ARDINGTON, WANTAGE, BERKSHIRE

Plate 58

PARGETTED COTTAGE, DATED 1697, AT CHIDDINGSTONE, NEAR EDENBRIDGE, KENT

AT WEST DRAYTON, NEAR UXBRIDGE, MIDDLESEX

Plate 59

AT ELHAM, NEAR FOLKESTONE, KENT

this pleasant treatment in Lavenham, Suffolk; several in Hertfordshire; on cottages at Steventon, Berkshire; Burford, Oxfordshire; in Northamptonshire; at Canterbury; and a few scattered examples elsewhere in Kent.

External plaster was also largely used on clay-lump walls of Norfolk and in other of the Eastern Counties, as well as to protect the cob walling and occasionally also the roughly built stone cottages of Devonshire and other counties in the South-West. It is not always easy to tell what is beneath the plaster especially where clay lump and wattle-and-daub were used in the same locality.

The present craze for stripping the protective coat of plaster is most unwise. Of course it was put for the very practical reason of making life inside these habitations more comfortable and warm by keeping out wind and rain. The uncovering fashion is only practised where it is desired to expose the oak timbers, but these have always been damaged by the insertion of numberless nails to make a key for the plaster. Even if all these are withdrawn the result is very untidy, for the timbers were of the roughest description when the original intention was to plaster them. Then to make matters worse—the stupidity of fashion again—oil is applied to the poor old injured " bones " after the " flesh " has been removed, and even creosote in the more extreme cases of stupidity and sheeplike mass thinking. The contrast between the dark timbers and the white intervening panels then becomes too pronounced and thoroughly unpleasant. As a consequence a modern restored look is the inevitable result and artistically the building is ruined. The old people knew better. This modern oiling nonsense is the greatest possible fallacy, but, unfortunately, it dies hard.

One of the secrets of old plaster was its thickness, and another was its toughness produced by the large amount of cow-hair used in its composition; the hair being scraped off the hides for this purpose, and *not* removed by the very doubtful new-fangled chemical process which is now the labour-saving but material-impairing process.

Chopped hay, or chopped straw, was sometimes substituted for the hair.

". . . When stone walls superseded wattle in North Wales," writes Mr. C. F. Innocent, " the stones were at first daubed like the wattle with a mixture of clay and cow dung. This had a wider range than North Wales and in England such important buildings as the churches were often daubed or plastered in the Middle Ages. As an instance the church of St. Michael, Bath, in the year 1394, was daubed with lime and sand, both inside and out ('tam infra quam extra '). . . ."[1]

Cow dung and road scrapings were used with the lime and sand in East Anglian pargetting.

Batty Langley's *London Prices*, of 1750, is quoted by Mr. Innocent as giving one fourth part of dung incorporated with the lime by well beating it, for pargetting.

Walls of mud were often made quite durable by their plastered finish in olden days.

According to Wm. Horman's *Vulgaria* (1519) ". . . Some men wyll have theyr wallys plastered, some pergetted, and whytlymed, some rough caste, some pricked, some wrought with playster of Paris. . . ." The pricked treatment, referred to by Horman, as also the scratched patterns, were equally the common finish to cottage exteriors all over Suffolk and Essex. Nothing looks better than this delightful Essex "stick-work," if well done, but the patterns produced should be small in scale and not too mechanically performed. It is difficult to find plasterers now to do such work, easy as it is and numerous as are the examples for them to follow. The tradition has been lost. The best period for

[1] *The Development of English Building Construction*, p. 143.

COTTAGES PLASTERED EXTERNALLY 45

plasterwork was from the beginning of the sixteenth century to the early part of the eighteenth century.

The pricked and scratched patterns gave a pleasant "all-overish" kind of texture to the surface and this has since been improved by repeated coats of whitewash which has the effect of making the patterns less obtrusive and pleasantly indefinite in places. Herring-bone, guilloche, scalloped fans and interlacing squares were the favourite patterns.

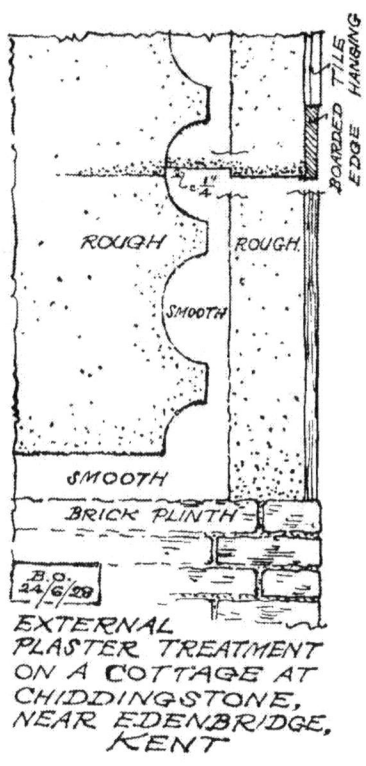

Fig. 20.

Another quite usual method was to panel the rough surfaces by forming narrow smooth divisions by pressing flat boards between, sometimes varied by diapering and other patterns, as seen in the symmetrical and somewhat formal little cottage, dated 1697, at Chiddingstone in Kent (Plate 58), a detail of which is given in Fig. 20. This treatment is comparatively rare in this county though another example, but of scroll form, is still to be seen in the gables of some cottages at Mereworth (pronounced "Merryworth"), near Maidstone. One of these is shown in Fig. 21. Presumably flat wooden or metal cut templates were formed, or partially formed, to the required design and were then pressed into the surface of the rough plaster, when moist, and manipulated somewhat after the fashion of those "aids to draughtsmen," known as French curves.

The separate central lozenge may have been produced

with a single mould, or with a mould for half only, but in two operations, to complete required shape.

A variation of this same pressed method is to be found at Nayland, Suffolk (Fig. 22).

Moderately wide flush mouldings were frequently used to bound the rectangular panels.

As in old modelled plaster ceilings, so in the external plastering or pargetting, the secrets of their charm are chiefly attributable to their variation in surface and texture, their lack of uniformity, and the freedom and spontaneity of the design, where ornament was used.

Another example from Kent — and a very fine one — is the dignified row of cottages at Elham, near Folkestone (Plate 59). Since Mr. Nathaniel Lloyd took his photograph the plastering has been removed, but, it must be admitted, with less disastrous results than usual. This building is rich in unusual detail, notably the moulded brick corbelling to the gable-end and the fifteen finely carved oak brackets. The doors and windows, of varied types and dates, are also of interest.

Fig. 21.—17th Century pargetting on a 15th Century building (now cottages) near Mereworth, Maidstone, Kent: an example of pressed scroll ornament.

Plate 60

AT BISHOPSTONE, NEAR AYLESBURY, BUCKINGHAMSHIRE

COTTAGE AT BISHOPSTONE: ANOTHER VIEW

Plate 61

AT MADINGLEY, NEAR CAMBRIDGE

AT WALKERN, NEAR STEVENAGE, HERTFORDSHIRE

COTTAGES PLASTERED EXTERNALLY 47

The series of cottages, illustrated by Plates 60 to 69, together with Plate 57 and the upper one of Plate 58, show the simplest form of plasterwork in East Anglia and the Home Counties, and include good examples from Norfolk, Suffolk, Cambs., Hunts., Essex, Herts., Beds., Bucks., and one from Middlesex (Plate 58), (to name the counties of origin north of the Thames), as well as a single specimen, of a very high order, from Berkshire.

The effect of sunlight and shadow on the whitewashed plaster of the little thatched cottage at Bishopstone, Bucks (Plate 60) is most alluring as also is the lovely Ardington cottage (Plate 57).

Roof forms and thatching mannerisms in Cambs., Hunts. and Essex have many points in common, as may be appreciated by reference to the plates.

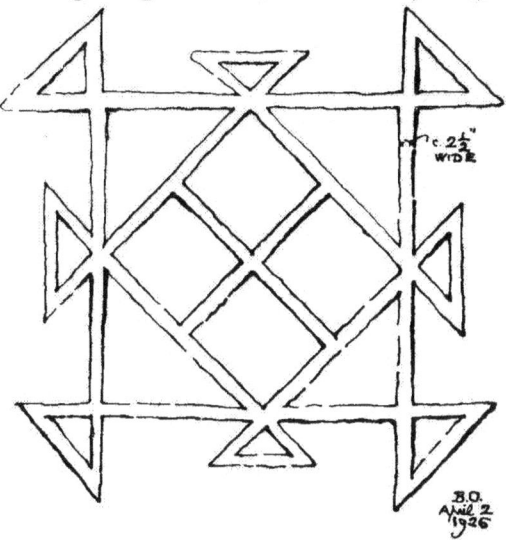

Fig. 22.—Late 17th Century pargetting ornament, of simple geometrical design, on a cottage, at Nayland, Suffolk.

The two groups of cottages (Plate 67), each, in opposite directions, within a few miles of Sudbury, Suffolk, have certain merits, for instance, the well-judged shape and pitch of the roofs of the Little Cornard cottages is very satisfying, but they are now in a sad state of disrepair through sheer neglect.

The Glemsford group, dated 1614, is of rather a different class. Although, at the present time, these too are cottages, this three-storied building was once used, many years ago, as a school. Its appearance could be greatly improved by re-opening the blocked windows, in all three gables and reglazing all the windows with leaded lights, as they were originally. The Jacobean staircase to the first floor and all but a few fragments of panelling have, unfortunately, been removed. Access to the attics has been blocked and the spacious roof is therefore wasted. The building stands high upon a hill and forms a conspicuous landmark.

A good example of the Essex " stick-work " treatment, already described, is to be seen in the overhanging gable of the cottages in Great Warley Street (Plate 69). The very pleasant texture produced by (in this case) herring-bone or zig-zag patterns, is just discernible in the illustration, but its full effect, softened and made a little indefinite by periodical white-washing, is more appreciable in actuality than in any photographic representation.

Quite apart from the question of plaster finish this is a good instance of the conspicuous success of unstudied accidental grouping, the different elements of architectural composition producing, oddly enough, complete harmony and repose. To have attempted to achieve such a result deliberately would have been well nigh impossible and courting almost certain failure.

In the clay-lump method of building adopted so extensively in Norfolk, Suffolk and Cambridgeshire, etc., walls were formed either in a solid piece or with clay lumps or bricks, reinforced with straw, well dried in the sun, and of varying sizes convenient for handling, but always larger than burnt bricks and similarly pressed into moulds.

A common size for clay bricks was eighteen or sixteen by six by nine inches. They were bedded in clay mortar, and, writes Mr. C. F. Innocent, ". . . were carried up in a rather rough manner to ensure key, and the angles were protected by angle beads. The plaster might be either of good clay mixed with road sand or silt, or, more frequently, of old

Plate 62

AT HILTON, NEAR ST. IVES, HUNTINGDONSHIRE

AT SAWTRY JUDITH, WEST OF RAMSEY, HUNTINGDONSHIRE

Plate 63

AT BRAMPTON, NEAR HUNTINGDON

AT MAULDEN, NEAR AMPTHILL, BEDFORDSHIRE

Plate 64

AT TOPSON, WRENINGHAM, NEAR WYMONDHAM, NORFOLK

BETWEEN HOLYWELL AND NEEDINGWORTH, NEAR ST. IVES, HUNTINGDONSHIRE

Plate 65

BARRINGTON, SOUTH-WEST OF CAMBRIDGE

BEAUMONT HILL, GREAT DUNMOW, ESSEX

Plate 66

WATER STREET, LAVENHAM, SUFFOLK
(See also Plate 56)

ICKLETON, CAMBRIDGESHIRE, NEAR GREAT CHESTERFORD, ESSEX

Plate 67

AT LITTLE CORNARD, NEAR SUDBURY, SUFFOLK
(AT FOOT OF SPOUT LANE, ON ROAD TO BURES AND COLCHESTER

IN LOW STREET, GLEMSFORD, NEAR LONG MELFORD, SUFFOLK: dated 1614
(THERE ARE BLOCKED WINDOWS IN ALL THREE GABLES)

COTTAGES PLASTERED EXTERNALLY

clay or loam and madgen, well kneaded with old straw to a proper consistency by being trodden by horses. Such a wall was raised two ft. above the surface of the soil, on a flint wall, called a pinning. The buildings were cheap, and they were warm in winter and cool in summer. . . ."[1]

Alternatively brick was used for the plinth which was sometimes tarred to make it more weatherproof. It will be observed that road scrapings were one of the important ingredients in well-made clay lumps just as they were in the composition of ornamental pargetting. With the increasing number of tar macadamed roads it would be difficult nowadays to find sufficient quantity of this important component part if ever any considerable revival in clay lump or pargetting occurred, but this is unlikely with so many modern building material substitutes available, and other methods from which to choose.

According to Mr. F. W. Troup ". . . Half the cottages in Norfolk that appear to be brick are really built of clay lumps faced afterwards (many quite recently) with $4\frac{1}{2}$ in. of brickwork. . . ."[2]

In Cambridgeshire even the protective external coat of plaster was often formed of a kind of chalk marl mixed with straw, a cheaper form of toughening it than cow-hair which was so generously used when the pargetting was to be ornamented in bold relief as well as for the more elaborate plaster ceilings of the seventeenth century. In the same county old walls have been found to consist of " clunch," which is a hardened form of chalk, and this has been banded with two or three layers of bricks, as in the original walls of Christ's College, Cambridge, but generally stone is rare in this area.

Occasionally the outside surface of clay walling was

[1] *The Development of English Building Construction*, p. 154.
[2] *The Arts Connected with Building*, p. 70.

merely covered with two or three good coats of lime, but in course of time, with almost annually repeated applications of thick limewash, this more economical method developed into quite a passable substitute for the more normal precedure.

Tar was also used in exposed positions but too much of it is ugly and apt to be depressing on large plain surfaces It is only a little less intolerable on weather-boarding where there is some light and shade variation. However it is done it is of the utmost importance—and indeed essential—that the clay should be protected externally, and kept absolutely watertight. Once water penetrates rapid disintegration is inevitable, just as with cob walling. Mr. Claude J. W. Messent, in his book on Norfolk, referred to elsewhere, mentions, " . . . the old process of an outer coat of a clay slurry topped with tar, sanded and colour-washed . . . sometimes pink and sometimes cream and white. . . ."[1]

Norfolk possesses some of the most suitable clay—especially where the boulder clay abounds in the south of the county—for making the lumps. It has been in use there more or less continuously since the beginning of the seventeenth century, but the probability is that it was still more general before the revived use of burnt bricks at that time. If well protected, it will last three hundred years or more. It is still used at the present day but with a surface finish of cement rendering—as, for instance, in modern Council houses at Blo' Norton and Garboldisham—in place of the old methods.

Mr. Messent's local knowledge lends value to the interest of his description of how the clay ". . . is first dug near the site where the building is to be erected and spread out in a layer about a foot thick. Stones larger than a walnut are removed. The clay is then watered and short straw or

[1] *The Old Cottages and Farm-houses of Norfolk*, p. 71.

ON THE STOUR AT FLATFORD, NEAR EAST BERGHOLT, SUFFOLK
(CONSTABLE'S COUNTRY)

grass is spread over it and trodden in by a horse, (as mentioned by Mr. Innocent) the straw being used as a binding agent. The clay having been thus prepared is then put into wood moulds or frames, and the block thus formed is generally eighteen inches long by nine inches wide by six inches deep; these are used for external walls only. Smaller blocks are usually eighteen inches long by six inches wide by six inches deep. The blocks are formed on level ground and left where made for three to four days, when they are generally sufficiently dry to be turned up on end and wheeled on a barrow to a platform where they are left to dry out. This generally takes a month or two, according to the season of the year. Sometimes the clay is raised in winter for use the following spring. . . ."[1]

Clom, clob, but more commonly cob, are dialect names for mud walls which it is known were in use in London as early as 1212, and about the country generally though we now particularly associate cob with Devon, and other Western counties.

The material had to be just right to stand. Mr. Innocent gives evidence from Dorset, Oxfordshire and Leicestershire in his book, of the use of road scrapings—as in the composition of clay lump and pargetting—for making the best walls of this type.

Sometimes straw and stubble was mixed with the mud and this was called tempering.

In Buckinghamshire walls were built of a kind of white clay, known as " witchit," found about eighteen inches below the surface of the ground.[2]

". . . Wet was a great enemy of cob walls, and in order to resist it and also the inroads of vermin, it was necessary to lay a foundation of stone. The cob should

[1] *Ibid*, p. 71.
[2] C. F. Innocent, *The Development of English Building Construction* p. 134, et seq.

project over the stone foundation about 1½ inches. There was a Devonshire saying that all cob wants is a good hat and a good pair of shoes, that is, a stone foundation and a coping of thatch . . . a usual protection for cob in the eighteenth century. Cob is very durable when properly protected, and in the middle of the last century in Devon, there were houses in perfect preservation which had been built in the reign of Elizabeth.

"In building the walls the only implements used were a dungfork and a " cob parer," which was like a baker's peel, the shovel for removing bread from the oven.

"The first layer of cob was built 2½ feet high all round the foundation and the walls themselves were 2 feet thick.

"The stuff was used as wet and soft as ordinary mortar, and after a week or so, according to the dampness or dryness of the atmosphere, allowed for the layer to consolidate, another layer was put on, and so on until the work was finished, two year's being required for a two storied house if it were to be properly done. In Devonshire each course was known as a 'raise.' When building a cob wall one of the workmen (known as a cob mason) stood on the wall to tread it down, and the woodwork, such as the lintels of doors and cupboards, was fixed in as the work went along. The walls had a tendency to crack, especially at the corners, and they were generally rounded to avoid this ; but this rounding of the corners may have had its origin in early circular or oblong buildings, and been retained for practical purposes. The cob also scaled off and bulged when the whitewash or plaster with which it was usually coated became decayed, and thus some Devon villages had an extremely dilapidated appearance a century ago. . . ."[1]

In those parts of Dorset and Hampshire where chalk was obtainable it was ground up and mixed with the cob which

[1] C. F. Innocent, *The Development of English Building Construction*, p. 134, et seq.

Plate 69

GREAT WARLEY STREET, NEAR BRENTWOOD, ESSEX

IN NEW STREET, HONITON, DEVONSHIRE

Plate 71

AT EAST LULWORTH, WAREHAM, DORSET

AT COOMBE CELLARS, ON RIVER TEIGN, NEAR NEWTON ABBOT, DEVONSHIRE

Plate 72

AT SCRIVELSBY, NEAR HORNCASTLE, LINCOLNSHIRE,
THE HOME OF THE KING'S CHAMPIONS

AT CLEEVE PRIOR, NEAR EVESHAM, WORCESTERSHIRE

COTTAGES PLASTERED EXTERNALLY

was greatly improved thereby. A usual proportion in the composition of the cob was three parts of chalk to one of clay, well kneaded and mixed together with straw.

Mr. Innocent explains how the composition of the cob varied according to county and the local materials available, and he instances the sandy and healthy districts of Dorset where ". . . loam, gravel and sand were used, and heath was used as a binding material instead of straw, but such cob was not as durable as that composed of chalk. In Cornwall cob was composed of two loads of clay to one load of shilf, that is broken slate in small pieces such as is used for mending roads, barley straw was added afterwards. Each 'raise' was diminished in height. . . ."[1]

The "spit and dab" work in cob buildings in West Somerset is more akin to the "wattle and daub" of East Anglia, but in both these types the reinforcement is far more elaborate, enabling quite thin walls to be built. These, however, are unlike the typical 2 ft. thick cob walls of the old thatched cottages of Devon, Dorset and Somerset (round about Minehead).

It is not too much to say that the charm of these annually whitewashed cob cottages with their tarred plinths, and their soft and unobtrusive gray thatched roofs, endears those counties to many of us more than anything else. They are essentially homely and comfortable and undoubtedly the most beautiful cottages in the world. They seem to express in their delightful simplicity the easy-going natures of the kindly folk who built and inhabited them.

Concerning the three remaining plates in this section of the book, and before considering Plate 70, it might be well firstly to turn back to the last illustration of Chapter I (Plate 40) when it will be seen that at Hallaton, in Leicester-

[1] C. F. Innocent, *The Development of English Building Construction.*

shire the top finish of a pair of two-tiered bay-windows is not altogether satisfactory.

This problem is always a difficult one for the architect, and in this case the thatch comes down very awkwardly over the bays.

On the other hand the wide overhang of roof to the very attractive Honiton cottages (Plate 70) makes it possible for the bays to run right up to the soffit of eaves and for the rain water gutter to be carried continuously along the foot of the thatch. This makes an infinitely better job. The two methods are well worth comparing. The bays of the weather-boarded cottages at Hawkhurst, Kent (Plate 79) also finish satisfactorily under the eaves.

There are a good many factors that contribute to the success of this long low little Honiton building; firstly, the charming effect of light and shade (when the sun is shining, as it shone in the early hours of the summer morning when the photograph was taken); secondly, the happy form of the bays; thirdly, the reduction in size of the upper windows; fourthly, horizontality of the casement windows, complete with their presumably original leaded lights; fifthly, the absence of windows between the bays; sixthly, the simple door-hoods with their shaped supports; and lastly, the uneven surface of the plastered wall with its high tarred plinth. The doors themselves are evidently semi-modern.

Typical West Country cob and thatch building in Dorset and Devon, delightful to look upon and in delightful surroundings, are shown on Plate 71.

The concluding examples of whitewashed cottages, from counties as wide apart as Lincolnshire and Worcestershire, are paired together on Plate 72. The single specimen—and the only one in this book—of topiary, in the cottage-garden at Cleeve Prior, shows what a picturesque asset clipped yews can be, whatever be the status of the architectural background.

PLATE 73

AT SMEETH, NEAR ASHFORD, KENT

AT BREWER STREET, BLETCHINGLEY, NEAR REDHILL, SURREY

CHAPTER IV

TIMBER-FRAMED AND PARTLY BRICK-BUILT COTTAGES, TILE-HUNG AND WEATHER-BOARDED

Mostly found in Kent, Sussex and Surrey—Illustrations from these three South-Eastern Counties.

TILE-HANGING, on old buildings, is rare north of Surrey, Kent and Sussex. There is an exception at Takeley, Essex, on a cottage near the railway, but it is difficult to recall any other old example in the Eastern Counties, except an isolated instance at Dereham, in the middle of Norfolk.

In the south-east of England its use—as that of weather-boarding—is general, and it is perhaps the most marked characteristic of the three first named counties.

Where the tiles used are plain, with specially made angle-tiles, the effect is more restful but there are numbers of examples of the rounded, or " fish-scale " pattern and other more fanciful varieties. For numerous reasons these ornamental tiles are almost tolerable in old work though they invariably give a commonplace look when used on a new building, in their modern form of too great perfection of shape, texture and colour.

Some such form of protection to the outer face of the timber-framed buildings in the exposed neighbourhood of the south coast is very necessary and effective in preventing rain from penetrating their thin walls, (only five to six inches thick), or even thicker walls of porous underburnt bricks. No more agreeable method has ever been devised of meeting "Nature's challenge." Slate-hanging in Lakeland, Cornwall, Normandy and Brittany; pargetting in East Anglia; and weather-boarding, were all used for the same purpose. Nowadays we pin our faith too often to eleven-inch hollow walls.

Sometimes patterns were produced by using plain square-edged tiles of different shades in a variety of diaper forms.

According to Mr. Curtis Green, ". . . The tiles for this purpose were sometimes of the same make and colour when they left the potter's hands, the pattern developing only with age; one lot of the tiles forming the pattern had been dabbed with the bristles of a stiff brush before the tiles were burnt, thus producing a rough surface which weathered more quickly than the ordinary hand-made tile. Weather tiles were hung on oak laths and were bedded solid in lime and hair mortar," and "were fastened with pins of hazel or willow, and sometimes of elder. . . ."[1] Nowadays copper nails are most favoured for the purpose because of their lasting quality, as also for roofing with tiles and slates. Fir battens are unsuitable as they split when nails are driven into them.

Roofing tiles used by the Romans in England were of Italian pattern, but the origin of plain tiles used in English mediæval buildings is rather obscure. A Statute of Edward IV (in 1477) regulated the size of tiles to be $10\frac{1}{2}$ in. by $6\frac{1}{4}$ in. by $\frac{5}{8}$ in. thick, and this has been the approximate size right up to the present day.

Tiles were, however, rather in the nature of a luxury until the seventeenth century owing to their cost of production, necessitating coal or wood fuel. Thatch generally

[1] *Old Cottages and Farmhouses in Surrey*, pp. 26 and 27.

Plate 74

THE GREEN, GROOMBRIDGE, NEAR TUNBRIDGE WELLS, KENT

THE WALKS, GROOMBRIDGE

GROOMBRIDGE: VIEW OF THE WALKS FROM OPPOSITE END

Plate 75

AT CHIDDINGFOLD, NEAR GODALMING, SURREY

AT MAYFIELD, SUSSEX
(BETWEEN HAILSHAM AND TUNBRIDGE WELLS)

Plate 76

AT WITLEY, NEAR GODALMING, SURREY

AT LIMPSFIELD, SURREY
(See also Plate 91)

Plate 77

AT NINE ELMS, MILFORD, NEAR GODALMING, SURREY

NORTH END COTTAGES, HAMPSTEAD, LONDON
(NOTE: THESE COTTAGES HAVE BEEN DESTROYED)

TILE-HUNG AND WEATHER BOARDED 57

was then the normal roof covering except in the stone districts where stone slates came naturally to hand.

Tile-hanging is to be seen at its best in the charming village of Groombridge near Tunbridge Wells, Kent (Plate 74). Here indeed is a village, with its Green and Walks, lime trees and lovely little eighteenth century cottages and shops, that ought to be preserved inviolate, for they together form a priceless and unique possession. Note how extraordinarily well the sash windows and casement windows and hipped dormers all blend. In the top view, nothing is straight nor regular and the mellowness of age greatly contributes to all their other attractive qualities.

The cottage at Smeeth, near Ashford in the same wonderful county—*facile princeps* in architectural interest in the whole of England—is thoroughly typical of the less formal class of cottage. This, with the cottage at Brewer Street, Bletchingley, Surrey (both on Plate 73) have certain points of resemblance with the third of the South-Eastern group of counties, i.e., Sussex, as can be seen by comparing them with Plates 75, 76 and 77.

Where timber-framed walling is covered with horizontal boards of oak or elm—and sometimes the whole external walls of a house—are so protected, but more often only the upper part above a brick-built ground floor—this method is known as weather-boarding.

The lower part of Plate 77 shows an example of London weather-boarding. These North End Cottages in Hampstead now, unfortunately, no longer exist, but they are a pleasant reminder of the minor domestic architecture of the eighteenth century. A few others of rather humbler character yet remain in South London, and by or near the Thames but their prototypes are still fairly numerous in Essex, Kent and other of the Home Counties.

In the North, for instance in South Lancashire, weather-boarding had been gradually replaced by stone walls by the beginning of the eighteenth century but its survival in the South may be attributable to the milder climate.

In the Eastern Counties, especially in Essex, since the fifteenth century, or even earlier, such boarding was also largely used for both windmills and watermills, but the former, alas! are fast disappearing. In that county it is occasionally found in bell turrets of churches, and in most cases is usually painted white.

In districts where the weather was more severe, as in Norfolk, tar was frequently applied instead of white paint, especially for farm buildings and the like. At the present time we compromise in our preservative treatment by using creosote. In recent years waney-edged elm-boarding has gained considerable favour, but unless used sparingly, and with taste and discrimination, it is apt to look tiresome. One of its drawbacks is its tendency to twist, and another is endwise shrinkage. It should be $\frac{3}{4}$ in. to 1 in. thick, and should be given a lap or at least 3 in.

At Little Dunmow, Essex, on a picturesque group of old cottages, one can see the application of weather-boarding, but the examples herein illustrated are chiefly from Surrey, Kent and Sussex.

Those on Plate 78, the one pair at Northiam, in East Sussex, and the other at Groombridge, in Kent, are very much alike in shape, so happily formed by the long flanking lean-to roofs. At Northiam the attic windows come in the white-painted weather-boarded gable-ends, whereas the bed-rooms in the Groombridge cottages are lit by square-topped dormers. Here the gable-ends are tile-hung without any visible break between the vertical face and the lean-to roofs at the lower level. The continuous drip-board, supported by shaped brackets over doors and windows is another pleasant feature of these same cottages.

Plate 78

WEATHER-BOARDED COTTAGES, AT NORTHIAM, EAST SUSSEX

THE BLUE COTTAGES, GROOMBRIDGE, NEAR TUNBRIDGE WELLS, KENT

Plate 79

ON THE ROAD TO WHATLINGTON, FROM BATTLE, SUSSEX

AT HAWKHURST, NEAR CRANBROOK, KENT

TILE-HUNG AND WEATHER BOARDED

Mr. Nathaniel Lloyd's cottages at Northiam, however, score a point in the little bonnet-tiled hips which unite the main roof with the tops of the end roofs. Of course one of the secrets of the success of this delightful little building is the steep pitch of the main roof. Other contributing factors are the dignified simplicity of the two chimneys and the diminution in size of the first floor windows—tucked neatly under the eaves—from the more important sitting room windows which come below them. Another point to notice is the thoughtful way the nearer end-chimney is purposely built out of centre with the ridge so as to permit of a reasonably sized two-light window being inserted in the gable-end, to one side of it. The rest of this large roof area is gable or dormer-lighted on the far side, of which no view is given.

The upper subject of Plate 79, on the road to Whatlington, from Battle, Sussex, shows that the introduction of a small portion of tile-hanging in the gable-end, while the rest of the upper part of the building is boarded, is not an uncongruous mingling of the two materials.

The boarded and bay-windowed cottages below, at Hawkhurst, Kent, have a good deal more architectural character. Many others, similar to these two types, are to be found in and about Smarden, but few have so satisfactory a quality of horizontality as the Hawkhurst group.

CHAPTER V

BRICKWORK AND FLINTWORK

Renewed use of bricks after timber became scarce—Revival of brickmaking in 15th and 16th centuries—Influence of Great Fire of London on popularity of bricks—Paucity of good examples—First introduced in Eastern Counties—Some East Anglian types of brick and brick-and-flint—Foreign influences in Norfolk and Suffolk—Larger size of bricks during period of brick tax—Survival of flint mining and knapping from prehistoric times—Brick-and-flint Gables—Chimneys of East Anglia compared with those in South-Eastern group of counties—Brick-and-stone cottages—Examples of different uses of brick from Herts., Norfolk, Suffolk, Lincs., Yorks., Glos., Hants., Bucks., Dorset and Wilts.

BRICKS are now the most universal of building materials, but it was not so in the past when timber was cheap and abundant. The great cottage-building period occurred before the scarcity began to be felt.

Good examples of brick-built cottages—mostly of the late seventeenth and eighteenth centuries—are comparatively rare, though their numbers are greater in Norfolk and Suffolk. In those counties brick was used more often for quoins and for straightening up the sides of door and window openings than by itself. The general walling in those cases was of flints which were so plentiful in East Anglia.

Lacing courses of thin square bricks, only about an inch thick, and more in the nature of tiles, were used by the Romans, Saxons and Normans in this country to strengthen their stone walls, but these bricks were usually of Roman make. There is a hiatus in the history of brick-making in

BRICKWORK AND FLINTWORK

England between Roman times and the thirteenth century when bricks were used in the construction of two East Anglian buildings which wholly, or in part, remain to the present day. These are Little Wenham Hall, Suffolk, and St. Nicholas' Chapel, at Coggeshall, in Essex. The first-named is the more interesting and intact, but in neither is there any evidence that the bricks were of native manufacture. It is thought by some authorities that they may have been imported. There is no doubt, however, that bricks were used in the eastern counties some time before they were elsewhere.

This is attributable to two causes (*a*) the lack of stone in East Anglia and (*b*) the proximity of the Netherlands, making importation easy. With regard to the second cause it was not only bricks but ideas that were imported from the Low Countries, as can be seen in the strong Flemish character of the more important brick buildings of the sixteenth and seventeenth centuries in Norfolk and Suffolk.

Professor Thorold Rogers has established, from his examination of mediæval building accounts, that bricks were used in the fifteenth century but, as he has pointed out, they were far too costly for general use at that early date.

It was really the Great Fire of London that gave the greatest impetus to brick-making and scared Londoners into the use of bricks in the great rebuilding after 1666. Thus did bricks come into fashion again. Their use has been constant and increasing ever since.

The worst period, both in the manufacture and laying of bricks, was the early nineteenth century, but the scope of this book does not extend beyond the good period.

The proportion of the bricks now in general use is much the same as the old ones, their length varying from $8\frac{1}{2}$ ins. to 10 ins., 9 in. being about the average. In breadth $4\frac{1}{2}$ in., $4\frac{3}{4}$ in., and even 5 in., are found, the first dimension being the most usual. At Little Wenham, the bricks were only $2\frac{1}{4}$ in. high, but old bricks rarely exceed $2\frac{1}{2}$ in. in height. For the duration of the brick tax (1784-1850) they were unfortunately made larger, with conspicuous detriment to the appearances of the buildings erected during that period.

Mr. Nathaniel Lloyd, in his fine book on brickwork, has pointed out that " . . . Most of the records of brickmakers refer to men bearing English names, but it is more than probable that they were employers of Flemish workmen, just as Michael Warrewyk received payment for bricks made by ' fflemyngs.' Further, there is no reason to suppose the bricks of which these buildings were constructed were made from any other than the local brick earths ; on the contrary, they usually bear every appearance of such origin. . . ."[1]

In Norfolk, brick and flint, in conjunction, were used more than any other building material, though on the west side of the county most of the buildings are of the local carstone, somewhat depressingly brown in colour. Elsewhere in Norfolk, but very generally throughout the rest of East Anglia, are found clay lump, wattle and daub, etc.

Mr. Claude J. W. Messent, refers to ". . . the yellow bricks," which he writes, " weather very well and are to be seen to their best advantage in villages where the chalk ridge gives way to the Fen country, as at Northwold, Methwold, Feltwell, Stoke Ferry, Wretton, etc. . . ."[2]

Old thick tiles, made from the same clay, such as can be seen in King's Lynn, have a very pleasing appearance when weathered by age. Mr. Messent describes how a maximum amount of oxide of iron in the clay produces a brick of dark red colour, in the same way as it affects the carstone, but where lime predominates in the earth a white brick is pro-

[1] *A History of English Brickwork*, p. 15.
[2] *The Old Cottages and Farm-houses of Norfolk*, p. 12.

PLATE 80

AT BAWBURGH, WEST OF NORWICH, NORFOLK

AT SOUTH COVE, NEAR SOUTHWOLD, SUFFOLK

Plate 81

AT HADHAM FORD, NEAR LITTLE HADHAM, HERTFORDSHIRE

COTTAGE, WITH STEPPED GABLE, AT BAWBURGH, WEST OF NORWICH, NORFOLK

Plate 82

HEACHAM GREEN, NEAR HUNSTANTON, NORFOLK

duced, hence the much over-rated and even ugly "White Suffolks."

Greater skill in the use of brick was shown in some of the old seaside cottages of Kent than along the the coasts of Norfolk and Suffolk. Note the pleasant diapering in the Broadstairs gable (Fig. 23).

Fig. 24 shows typical Norfolk gable-ends, one being from an elevation, measured and drawn by the late John S. Corder, of an old cottage at Potter Heigham, near Hickling Broad; and the other a perspective-sketch inset of a similar cottage at St. Olaves, close to Fritton Decoy. Both examples being in East Norfolk — N.W. and S.W. of Great Yarmouth—show pronounced Flemish influence.

Fig. 23.—Diapered Gable in High Street, Broadstairs, Kent. J. P. Seddon, *del*.

The brickwork to gable-parapets of both cottages is of the kind known as "tumbled in." At Potter Heigham an additional interest to the colour and texture has been obtained by the patterning of burnt bricks. An ovolo-moulded brick course gives a finish to the high plinth of flint rubble, with its brick quoins; and similar bricks are discernible where the brickwork is corbelled out to stop the ends of the eaves of the reed-thatched roof. Pantiles, which are so ubiquitous in Norfolk, are indicated in the St. Olaves sketch.

Fig. 24.—Old Cottage at Potter Heigham, Norfolk: Measured Detail of Gable-end.

BRICKWORK AND FLINTWORK

Compare the marked regional characteristics in Norfolk villages so wide apart as Bawburgh, near Norwich; Heacham, near Hunstanton; and Happisburgh, near North Walsham (Plates 80, 81, 82 and 83), and in the Suffolk village of South Cove, near Southwold (Plate 80).

In the charming thatched cottage at Happisburgh (locally pronounced "Hazeborough"), flint rubble is predominant.

The picturesque group at Hadham Ford, near Bishop's Stortford, Hertfordshire (the right hand in Plate 81) though thoroughly East Anglian in feeling —notably the pair of octagonal chimney-shafts,— is dissimilar to Norfolk cottages and those near to the Suffolk coast. Concerning the design of brick chimneys that (Fig. 25) on Mill Tye Cottages, Great Cornard, near Sudbury, Suffolk, is of interest because it is of a very effective seventeenth-century type, with flues more or less diagonally arranged on plan. There are many of these, with minor variations, to be found mostly in Suffolk, Essex, Herts., Cambs., and Hunts.

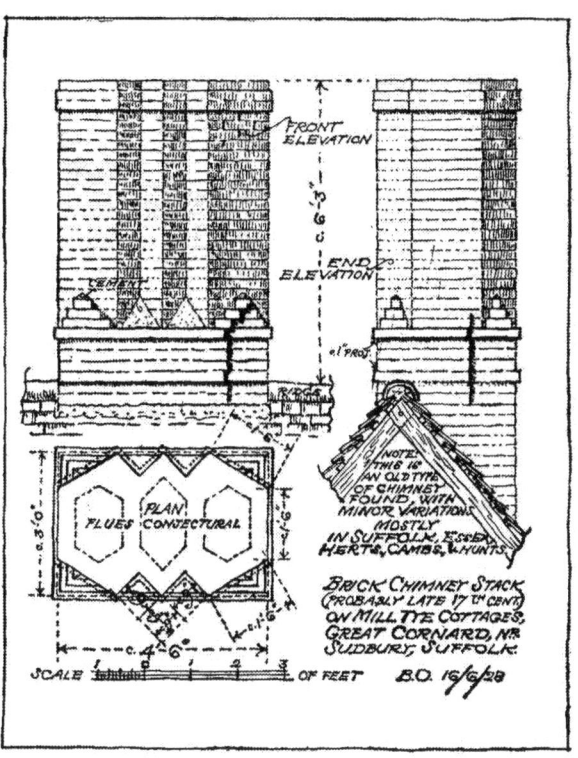

Fig. 25.

Kent and Sussex chimneys with their irregular plans—as opposed to the East Anglian symmetrical arrangement of flues illustrated in Fig. 25—are shown in the details of two stacks near Tenterden, Kent (Fig. 26). Corbelled and moulded brick caps of this kind are fairly general all over Kent, Sussex and Surrey, though each county, and even each village has often its own favourite.

In Surrey, for instance, as Mr. W. Curtis Green has noted. ". . . The variety of treatment of the chimney-stacks themselves is almost endless, and it is not easy to find two exactly alike, except in the same village. . . . Occasionally the flues are contained in separate shafts rising from the same base, which give lightness and beauty to the whole. More frequently many flues are built in one stack, sometimes regular and sometimes irregular in plan. . . ."[1] Mr. Green also draws attention to the large size of the flues. ". . . Never less than 9 inches by 14 inches, sometimes a

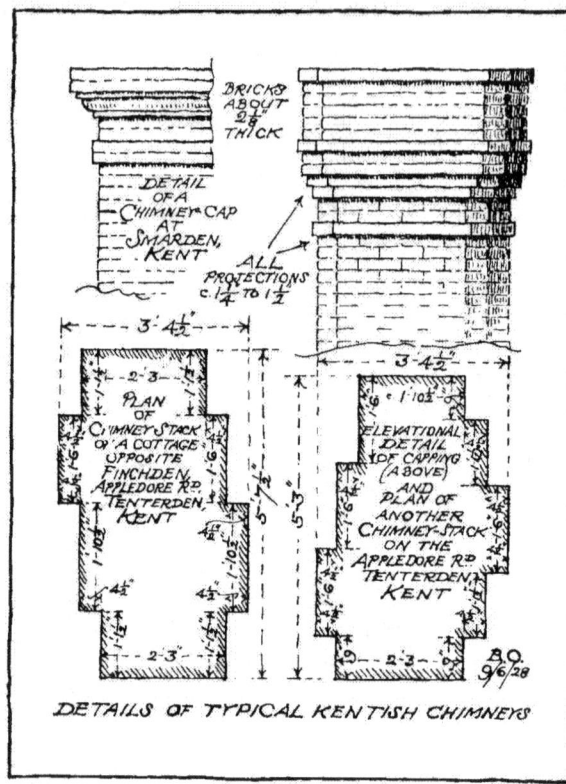

Fig. 26.

[1] *Old Cottages and Farm-houses in Surrey*, pp. 53, 54 and 55.

Plate 83

AT HAPPISBURGH, NEAR NORTH WALSHAM, NORFOLK

Plate 84

AT FRODINGHAM, NEAR SCUNTHORPE, LINCOLNSHIRE

AT BOLTON PERCY, NEAR TADCASTER, YORKSHIRE
(COTTAGES NOW PULLED DOWN)

great deal more, . . ." and to the fact that the outer skin is rarely more than half-a-brick thick, whereas it should be a whole brick (9 inches) thick, according to modern standards of good building.

Not only do old flues that are too large defeat the object of fireplaces, but that defect, coupled with a too thin outer skin, conduces to down-draught troubles.

It is true that such chimneys have great external dignity and charm but these virtues are better achieved by flues of merely adequate size with thicker weather-resisting outer skins; in other words by reversing the proportions of our forefathers.

Further north, but still on the east side of England, one finds cottages like that at Frodingham, near Scunthorpe, Lincolnshire (Plate 84), which demonstrates most effectively the attractive appearance of white-washed brickwork. Incidentally the value of limewash as a waterproofing medium—provided that the lime has been slacked in *boiling* water—cannot be too often emphasised.

The Bolton Percy group, near York, on the same plate has, unfortunately, disappeared.

Plate 85 shows a comparative rarity in Gloucestershire, an old example of brick and thatch at Frampton-on-Severn, where the thatch is brought down to form porch-roofs in a very ingenious manner. With its companion picture a comparison is afforded between the west and east of England, that of the latter also being brick-built with a thatched roof. It is at Flatford (near East Bergholt), the birthplace of Constable, on the Stour. That great artist must have been very familiar, in his youth, with this picturesque little cottage, and it is not improbable that he may even have sketched it.

The example from King's Worthy near Winchester, is typical of Hampshire cottage-building (Plate 87).

The windmill in the view below it, of the Buckinghamshire village of Quainton, adds to the composition of the group, but the brick cottages themselves have a quiet simplicity and dignity of their own.

From Morden, Dorset, and Lake, Wiltshire (together on Plate 86) we have two good West Country examples of the use of brick in which is rather unusual in old cottages in those counties of abundant stone, chalk and flint. In the Lake cottages, flint and stone have been used in association with brick quoins in a highly satisfactory manner.

There are many similar examples of this sparing use of bricks, merely limited to quoins, surrounds to door and window openings and horizontal bonding courses, in buildings of chalk, stone and flint, in eastern Wiltshire, near the Hampshire border, where bricks were close at hand.

In villages such as the Winterbournes, Codford St. Mary and Stratford-sub-Castle the wonderful texture obtained by haphazard but highly skilled mixture of materials can be seen.

Mr. Sydney R. Jones, whose knowledge of old cottage architecture is as great as his skill in depicting it, has drawn attention to the traits of this region, and he has noted that ". . . Extreme simplicity, combined with solidity of construction, was observed in both plans and elevations; the methods employed and materials used were not adopted to richness or complexity of detail, and the local builders rightly confined themselves to the just limitations of their work. Flint is found with the chalk, and this material is of predominant interest. It is responsible for a style of building as individually distinctive and local as may be found in England. The work is, in some measure, akin to that of Kent and the Eastern Counties; but while continental influence is largely traceable in the east, the guiding inspiration in Wiltshire was of a purely English origin. . . . A style of building was adopted, the character of which was almost wholly governed by the materials; flint for the one part, and for the other stone or brick, or both introduced in conjunction. . . . It was produced entirely by a common-sense use of material, acted and reacted upon the traditional ways and means. . . ."[1] (Refer back to Plate 26 of Fisherton-de-la-Mere, Wiltshire, where brick gives place to stone and it and flints occur chequer-wise).

In conclusion one ought to refer to East Anglian flintwork. In the western parts of both Norfolk and Suffolk flints have, for centuries, been used more largely than any other kind of building material. Indeed in the locality of Brandon, in the north-west corner of Suffolk, and on the borders of Norfolk, flint has been mined and *knapped* (i.e. chipped) for ornamental facing work of churches or for use as gun-flints, since prehistoric times.

The fashioning of arrow-heads, scrapers and other primitive implements constituted, of course, the original industry of over two thousand years ago. Most akin to these are the gun-flints which are still made in small quantities for the natives of some of our more remote Colonies. It was the best of the even black flint that was used for church building in the Eastern Counties in the fourteenth and fifteenth centuries. It is now very rarely required for that purpose though it might well be used. A revival of an old method need not necessarily imply the copying of old designs. The possibilities of decorative flintwork in a modern building can be seen to advantage in Sir Herbert Baker's use of this material in the War Memorial Cloisters at Winchester College, but such fine craftsmanship is obviously too costly for cottage building. For that purpose naturally the commonest and cheapest form of flintwork is rubble walling, consisting of surface flints of irregular

[1] *The Village Homes of England*, Special Spring Number of The Studio, 1912, pp. 20-25.

shape and size, used just as found, whether dark or light. These are known as cobbles.

" . . . Some flint cottages have small flint chips inserted in their mortar joints, which practice," writes Mr. Claude J.W. Messent, " is known as ' galleting ' or ' garreting,' and was done partly for strengthening purposes and partly as a method of decoration. . . ."[1] It gave a more even black surface as well as consolidating the mortar.

In this connection it is interesting to compare a similar custom elsewhere, referred to by that keen student of folk-building, Mr. Alfred H. Powell, who mentions that " . . . In Yorkshire they had a way of shielding their mortar joints by the use of ' pinners,' in Surrey called ' garnetting.' It consists in pushing little pieces of wetted stone into the finished jointing of the wall which, while it adds a kind of embroidery to the appearance, helps to retard the drying of the mortar . . ."[2] which, according to one tradition, is best when mixed with soft water.

[1] *The Old Cottages and Farm-houses of Norfolk*, p. 50.
[2] *Country Building and Handicraft in Ancient Cottages and Farm-houses*, The Studio Year Book, 1920, p. 30.

Plate 85

AT FLATFORD, EAST BERGHOLT, SUFFOLK

AT FRAMPTON-ON-SEVERN, NEAR STROUD, GLOUCESTERSHIRE

AT MORDEN, NEAR WAREHAM, DORSET

AT LAKE, ON THE AVON, NORTH OF SALISBURY, WILTSHIRE

PLATE 87

AT QUAINTON, NEAR AYLESBURY, BUCKINGHAMSHIRE

AT KING'S WORTHY, NEAR WINCHESTER, HAMPSHIRE

CHAPTER VI

FEATURES AND DETAILS

Chimneys—Slate-hanging and other weather-resisting precautions—External Staircases—Doorways—Windows of different types—Wrought Ironwork—Glazing—Gardens, and old writers on their Charm—Dry-walling and Thatched Walling—Thatch, its advantages and disadvantages, methods, and necessary precautions—Advice by old and modern writers.

FEATURES and the small details of old cottages are often of great interest. Of these, chimneys are perhaps the most prominent. Those of brick (Figs. 25 and 26) have already been referred to in the previous chapter, but less usual are the massive external chimney-breasts, terminating with cylindrical shafts found chiefly in Somerset and in the Lakeland districts of Westmorland and North-West Lancashire. Two sketches of these from Townend, Troutbeck, Windermere, are shown in Fig. 27. Here, unlike the usual Somerset practice, the flues are taken up in internal chimney-breasts which are less vulnerable to the weather. Rough-casting and numerous drips, to throw off rain from the walls, are further significant indications of the severity of the prevailing local climatic conditions.

Slate-hanging is equally effectual in resisting driving rain. Plate 88 illustrates two examples of this from Hawkshead in the same region. External staircases, such as here also shown, are occasionally met with in this curiously detached part of Lancashire which should normally be Westmorland but, for some obscure reason is not.

A much rarer feature is the picturesque little spinning-gallery, with its turned wood balusters, at Hartsop, Westmorland (Plate 89). This seems to breathe the very spirit of the Lake District by reason both of the scenery and the regional character of the building which are so marked that the subject hardly needs a title to tell its situation.

The typical street in the fishermen's quarter of St. Ives, Cornwall (Plate 90), shows some affinity to Hawkshead.

Contrast with the foregoing the South-Eastern and West-Midland types of brick-nogged timber-framing exemplified by the delightful cottages at Limpsfield, Surrey, and Tong, Shropshire (Plate 91). The ample width of old cottage doorways is especially conspicuous in the former.

Fig. 27.

This same virtue is also to be seen at Landkey Newland, near Barnstaple, Devonshire (Plate 92) though here its sturdy frame and charmingly shaped head—so reminiscent of old Dutch and Flemish woodwork—is altogether unusual.

No modern architect could have devised a more romantic entrance than that from Tillington, near Petworth, Sussex (on the same Plate).

Plate 88

FLAG STREET, HAWKSHEAD, LANCASHIRE
(Note: Hawkshead is situated between the north ends of Coniston Water and Windermere)

EXTERNAL STAIRCASE AND VERTICAL SLATE-HANGING AT HAWKSHEAD, LANCASHIRE (IN LAKELAND)

Plate 89

SPINNING GALLERY AT HARTSOP, BETWEEN LAKES WINDERMERE AND ULLSWATER, WESTMORLAND

FEATURES AND DETAILS

Cottage windows were few and small, and only a small proportion were made to open, chiefly on account of the extra cost of casements as against fixed lights, which were merely lead-glazed without any ironwork except for the horizontal or vertical saddle-bars to which the lead glazing was fixed with strong wire. Ventilation by means of the ever open door and the enormous chimney flues was considered adequate.

Casement windows in stone-built cottages of course had stone mullions, either straight-chamfered, ovolo-moulded or slightly hollowed. At a later date, and in the brick and timbered parts of the country, wood frames, pegged together, were generally used. These windows gave a horizontal character to the buildings, but less so when transomes were introduced though these were usually in the larger houses.

Sash windows were an innovation from Holland in the seventeenth century and, by their very nature, inevitably led to a feeling of verticality in the design.

Plates 93, 94 and 95 illustrate windows of oriel type in timber-framed buildings and are picturesque variations from the more general flat form. Plate 93 also shows a good example of Cheshire "magpie" timbering which tells to greater advantage by being restricted to a single feature.

The moulded stone surrounds to doors and windows of the cottage, now used as the Post Office at Hampstead Marshall, near Newbury, Berkshire (Plate 96), show very markedly the influence of the Renaissance. Pleasant though these features are they might even be described as "architecty"—as compared with inherited building traditions which are exhibited in the other illustration from Harlestone, Northamptonshire, on the same page. There is fine masculine character about the last-named and it is a splendid example of dignified and completely satisfying horizontality.

The use of wrought iron in England has been continuous

for at least two thousand years and is still used (though for cheapness, more often in malleable form) for such purposes as window casements with their stays and ornamental fasteners, door-hinges, door-handles, knockers, railings, screens, gates, nails, inn-signs and the like, but until comparatively recent times it was, like lead, regarded as almost a precious metal. " . . . The old iron which remains is remarkable for its

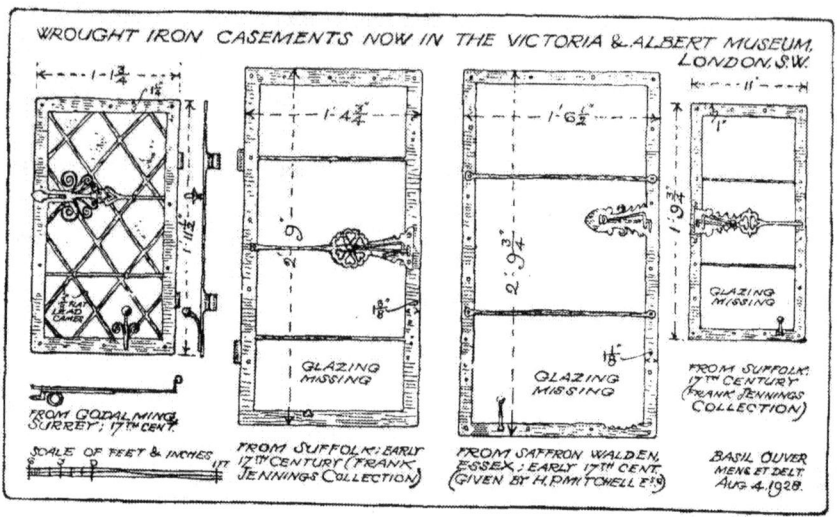

Fig. 28.

freedom from rust and for its lasting qualities and durability during periods of time in which modern iron would have decayed away. This is generally held to be due to the smelting of the old iron with charcoal instead of coal or coke. . . ."[1]

Our forefathers had nothing to learn with regard to fitness for purpose, and they knew intuitively how far to go in the beautification of the utilitarian, invariably performed with the nicest taste.

Such necessary fitness as casement-fasteners never fail

[1] C. F. Innocent, *The Development of English Building Construction*, p. 273.

PLATE 90

TYPICAL STREET IN THE FISHERMEN'S QUARTER, ST. IVES, CORNWALL

FEATURES AND DETAILS

to catch the eye, where they happily remain *in situ*, but a very great number have now found their way into our museums, or are in the possession of collectors. Four casements complete with their ornamental fasteners, and in one case having original leaded glazing, are to be seen in Fig. 28 (with some of their fasteners shown in greater detail in Figs. 29, 30 and 31), from examples in the Victoria and Albert Museum, London, from Surrey, Suffolk and Essex.

Infinite pains were taken and much imagination was shown by village blacksmiths in the fashioning of these casement-fasteners for their exceptionally conspicuous positions, silhouetted, as they were, against the light. The care and pleasure derived from their making can well be guessed when measured by the delight that old craftsmanship now gives us.

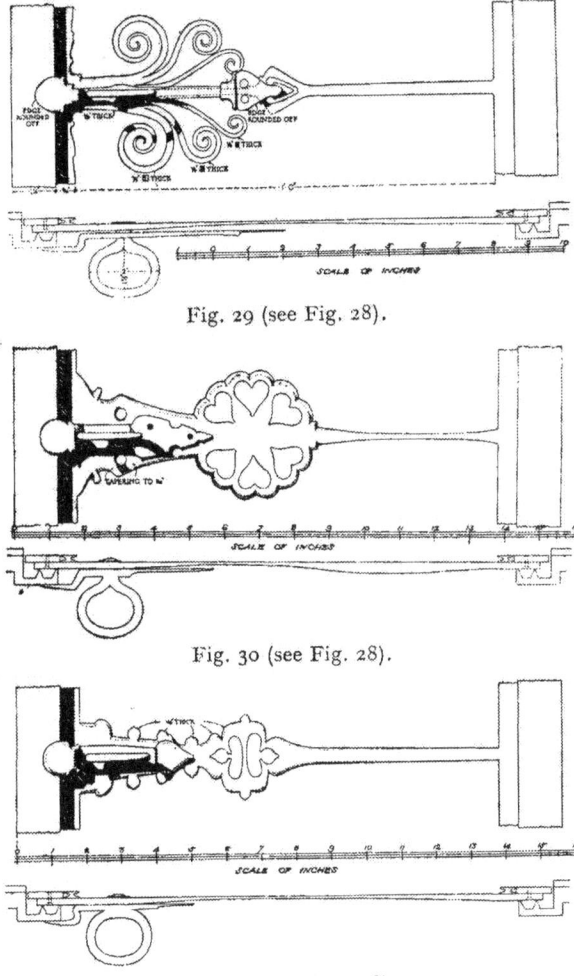

Fig. 29 (see Fig. 28).

Fig. 30 (see Fig. 28).

Fig. 31 (see Fig. 28).

That the smiths of the eighteenth century sometimes had a sense of humour, like their mediæval stone-carver predecessors, is exemplified by the ingenious and amusing sign bracket from the Fox Inn, Huntingdon (Fig. 32), now also in the Victoria and Albert Museum.

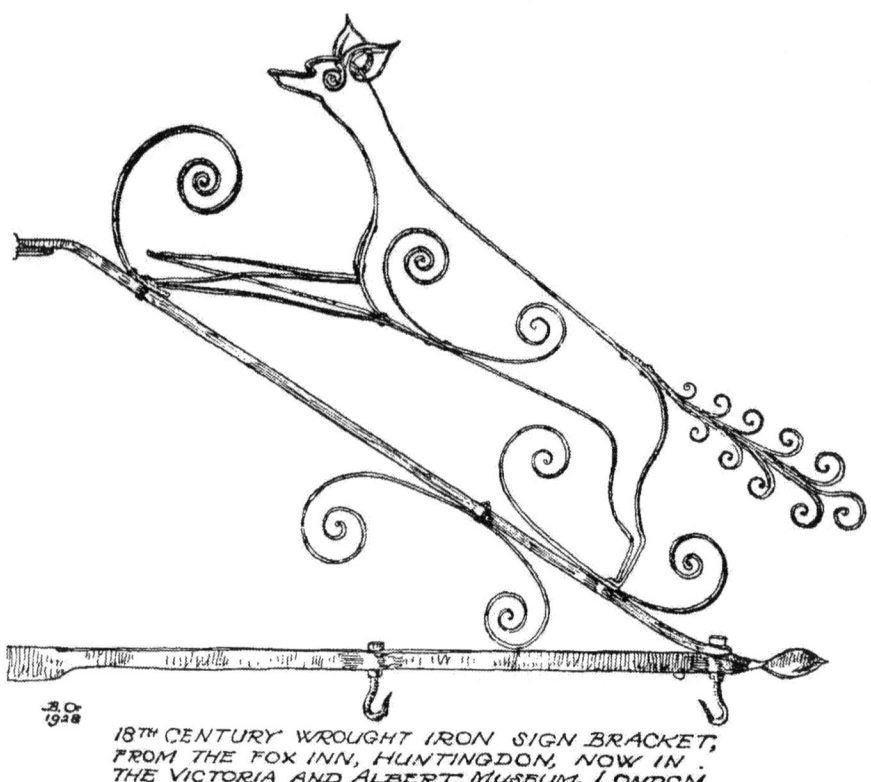

18TH CENTURY WROUGHT IRON SIGN BRACKET, FROM THE FOX INN, HUNTINGDON, NOW IN THE VICTORIA AND ALBERT MUSEUM, LONDON

Fig. 32.

In the few cottages left that still retain their original lead glazing, of " crown " glass, the external appearance of the building as a whole is thereby greatly enhanced.

The origin of diamond-shaped panes is not without interest. ". . . Early lattice windows were probably simply of upright twigs of branches, but it was found that cross-

Plate 91

AT LIMPSFIELD, SURREY
(See also Plate 76)

TIMBER, STONE, BRICK AND WHITEWASH AT TONG, SHIFNAL, SHROPSHIRE

Plate 92

DOORWAY AT LANDKEY NEWLAND NEAR BARNSTAPLE, DEVONSHIRE

DOORWAY AT TILLINGTON, PETWORTH, SUSSEX

Plate 93

AT NETHER ALDERLEY, EAST CHESHIRE

AT EAST HAGBOURNE, NEAR DIDCOT, BERKSHIRE

GABLES AT STEVENTON, dated 1657
(See also Plates 50 and 51)

CHIMNEY-STACK AT STEVENTON, NEAR ABINGDON, BERKSHIRE

FEATURES AND DETAILS

diagonal bars kept the rain out better. When lead-glazed windows took the place of the open lattice, the diagonal crossing of the lattice, according to established custom, was followed for the lead cames, and this is the origin of the common diamond-shaped panes. . . ."[1]

Rectangular panes came after the traditional form and as well as being more restful to the eye are, incidentally, less costly.

In rare cases the rigidity of rectangular glazing is relieved by curved variations at the head of the lights (see Fig. 33). We have many records of this pleasant fashion in seventeenth century paintings of Dutch interiors by Vermeer and others.

The detail of eaves treatment (Fig. 34), unusual for a cottage, shows the influence of the Renaissance in the seventeenth century. It is on the same building as the lead-glazing, just referred to, but it should be explained that it was the former Guest-house (though now two cottages), at Finchden, on the Appledore Road, near Tenterden, Kent.

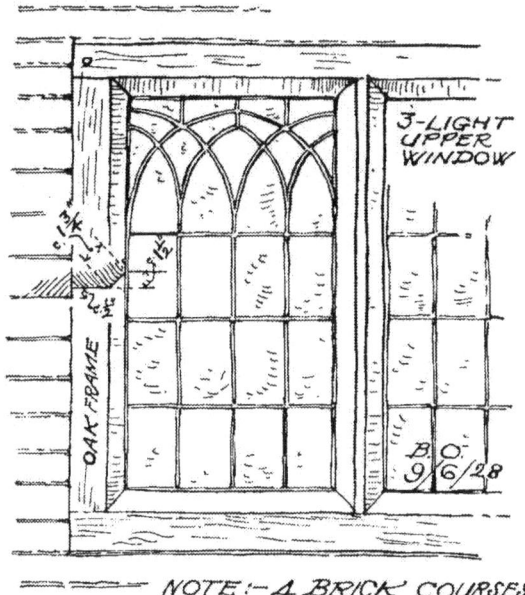

ORNAMENTAL LEAD-GLAZING IN 17TH CENTURY BRICK-BUILT GUEST-HOUSE (NOW COTTAGES) AT FINCHDEN, APPLEDORE ROAD TENTERDEN, KENT.

Fig. 33.

[1] C. F. Innocent, p. 256.

There is an elusive quality about cottage-gardens, and it is hard to define. The average villager was a born gardener and instinctively did what was right and appropriate in his gardening, with the result that his efforts invariably added to the attractiveness of his cottage-home.

Most often the garden is a narrow slip of ground with a long box-bordered path from the road-gate up to the front door. In the front garden flowers and vegetables are so cunningly arranged that even the latter are not unattractive. Where there is also a back garden it is usually devoted solely to vegetables which are so vital in making "ends meet" for the rural worker.

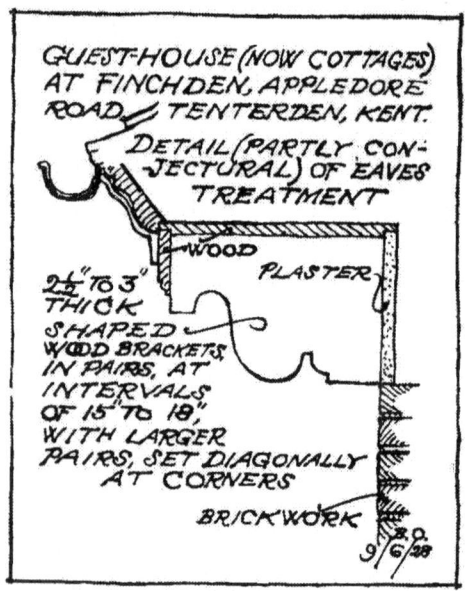

Fig. 34.

Plate 97 shows two characteristic Surrey examples, the one from Frensham and the other from Great Bookham.

The famous village of Elmley Castle, Worcestershire, provides an actual picture (Plate 98) of our dreams of what an old English cottage and garden should be.

Sir Henry Wotton, writing towards the end of James I's reign, refers to gardens as ". . . these externall delights," and he advises ". . . a certaine contrarietie between building and gardening: For as Fabriques should be regular, so gardens should bee irregular, or at least cast into a very wilde Regularitie. . . ."[1]

[1] *The Elements of Architecture*, collected by Henry Wotton, Knight, published in 1624.

FEATURES AND DETAILS 79

These are quite admirable sentiments and peculiarly applicable to cottage gardening now as then.

In this connection also perhaps an extract from a little poem, entitled, " The Garden," by one Abraham Cowley, written in the Merry Monarch's reign, may not come amiss, and might even be said to be redolent of that time. Thus it runs :—

> " Who that has reason and a smell
> Would not among Roses and Jesamine dwell,
> Rather then all his spirits choak,
> With Exhalations of dust and smoak,
> And all the uncleanness which does drown
> In pestilential clouds a populous town?
> The Earth itself breaths better perfumes here,
> Then all the semal men and women there
> (Not without cause it's thought) about them bear." [1]

This book would be incomplete without some reference to dry-walling, that is stone walls built without mortar, primarily used for marking the boundaries of fields and often for garden-walls in districts where stone abounds in such counties as Cornwall, Devonshire, Somerset, all over the Cotswolds and in most of the Northern Counties.

Mr. Alfred H. Powell has recorded that " . . . the dry-wallers of Gloucestershire still remember men who could build in a day, without hurry, twenty or thirty feet length of wall, eighteen inches wide and four feet six inches high, using no tool but a stone hammer which they threw at starting to measure out the day's work. . . ." [2]

Numbers of such walls are shown in the foregoing plates but particularly skilful pieces of herring-bone work are to be seen at Lee, near Ilfracombe, Devon (Plate 99), as

[1] Included in a collection of *Poems upon Divers Occasions*, selected by Jeremiah Wells and published in Oxford in 1667.
[2] *Country Building and Handicraft in Ancient Cottages* : The Studio Year Book, 1920, p. 29.

well as that enclosing the garden of the Old Post Office at Tintagel, Cornwall (Plate 20).

In other parts of the country, in Wiltshire and Berkshire for instance, are to be found farmyard and garden walls of cob, flint and stone, coped with protective thatch. One such example, at Blewbury, Berkshire is illustrated on Plate 99.

At the foot of the same page is an old cider mill, at Kilcot, near Newent, Gloucestershire, which has doubtless now given place to a more efficient but far less picturesque method of crushing apples.

In conclusion some consideration of thatch seems desirable for it is the oldest and most delightful of all roofing materials and upon it a great number of the subjects herein illustrated depend for their appeal. Conversely it is the absolute inappropriateness of incongruous modern roof-coverings—such, for instance, as pink asbestos—that has done so much to ruin the countryside. In this connection it is satisfactory to know that British manufacturers of asbestos tiles are not unmindful of the exceeding ugliness of some of the colours now used and that it is within the bounds of possibility that the manufacture of at least the offending pink variety might be discontinued, if only foreign makers could be brought into line, or if certain of their more disastrous products could somehow be excluded as "undesirable aliens." The gradual spoliation of our villages could be very considerably checked by some firm action of the kind.

Surely there can be no doubt which is the more beautiful, traditional steep-pitched thatched roofs of at least 50 degrees, or "would-be modern" flat roofs of the uncompromisingly ugly box-like buildings of Corbusier and his English imitators. Even the ultra-modernists must admit that there is no material comparable with thatch in making buildings become an integral part of the landscape. There is, however, some

Plate 95

ORIEL WINDOW AT WEST WYCOMBE, NEAR HIGH WYCOMBE, BUCKINGHAMSHIRE

(Note.—The village of West Wycombe has been purchased for preservation by The Royal Society of Arts)

ORIEL WINDOWS AT THEALE, READING, BERKSHIRE

Plate 96

DOORWAY TO POST OFFICE, HAMPSTEAD MARSHALL, NEWBURY, BERKSHIRE

COTTAGE AT HARLESTONE, NEAR NORTHAMPTON
(Note the pleasing horizontality of the composition)

prejudice against thatch on account of supposed fire dangers, and unfortunately high insurance premiums would appear to confirm the fear and tend further to deter people from its use, and so do bye-laws, though the latter are in some places happily now less rigid in this respect. But there really is no need for such timidity.

Mr. Alfred H. Powell, in a very informative article on the thatcher's craft, quotes cases known to him of " . . . A smithy near Cambridge upon which the sparks had fallen in thousands daily for seventy years without damage; and of a thatched house on fire in which the thatch refused to burn, finally falling upon and extinguishing the burning ruins." [1]

Reed thatch is the best and will last, without repair, for as long as thirty years. Buildings covered with thatch, especially of straw, should be kept in good repair and should not be placed too close to a road. It is a fact that thatch is more vulnerable from its underside, and for this reason it is a wise precaution, where the roof space is not used for attics and therefore not lath-and-plastered in the usual way, to protect the dry loose ends by boarding or asbestos sheeting or some such means.

Mr. G. Blair Imrie, in a very valuable defence of thatch, gives three principal causes of thatch fires, viz., defective flues; chimney fires; and the steam road vehicle. He points out that ". . . Almost all cottages and small houses built prior to 1800 had open fires; wood was used as fuel, and the walls of the chimneys were not severely tested. Gradually closed ranges and stoves came into use, and with their sharper draught and with coal as fuel the old flues (often leaky) became dangerous and fires resulted. . . ." [2]

To counteract this particular risk he recommends the use of fireclay pipes to line all flues in a thatched house but

[1] *The Architects' Journal*, Dec. 12, 1923, pp. 859–862.
[2] *Country Life : The Case for Thatch To-day*, Dec. 4, 1920, pp. 759, 760.

" . . . in all cases, whether flue pipes are used or not the chimneys should be carefully rendered in cement where they pass through the roof. . . ."

It is undeniable that thatch is warmer in winter and cooler in summer than other roofing materials. In this connection it is worth mentioning that when Mr. Imrie made a personal test he " . . . found that a reed-thatched house was about 10 degrees cooler in summer than a tiled house adjoining and," as he remarks, "it is no doubt correspondingly warmer in winter. . . ."

Thatch, in days gone by, was generally considered too humble a roof covering for anything but cottages, and in confirmation of this we know that Palsgrave in the year 1530 wrote " . . . I am but a poore man, sythe I can not tyle my house, I must be fayne to thacke it. . . ."[1]

But true cottages are poor men's homes, hence the reason why so many are thatched, but to us, of the present day, there was no need for Palsgrave to be apologetic. Quite the reverse.

True reed, so largely used in Norfolk, Suffolk and North Wales, is not only superior to the cultivated grasses but was probably used earlier.

Of the latter, "Rye straw was esteemed the best, because," as Mr. C. F. Innocent explains, " It was the longest and strongest. It was grown by some farmers solely for thatching, as it withstood wind, sun, rain, frost and snow. . . . Sometimes the top layer only was of rye. The next best was wheat straw, . . ."[2] though barley, oats and rye straw were also largely used, and these should be reaped with a sickle. Machine reaping damages the fibres of the straw and renders it unsuitable for thatching, as also does threshing.

[1] Quoted in C. F. Innocent's interesting chapter on *Thatching*, in *The Development of English Building Construction*, p. 190.
[2] *The Development of English Building Construction*, p. 191.

Plate 97

A COTTAGE GARDEN AT FRENSHAM, NEAR FARNHAM, SURREY

COTTAGE GARDENS AT GREAT BOOKHAM, LEATHERHEAD, SURREY

Plate 98

A COTTAGE AT ELMLEY CASTLE, NEAR EVESHAM, WORCESTERSHIRE

FEATURES AND DETAILS 83

It is important to wet the straw before it is used for thatching, if the work is to be done in Summer, but by tradition and experience of a thousand years, Autumn is considered the better time, and is more usual.

Henry Best, a farmer of Elmswell, in East Yorkshire, whose instructions for thatching, written in 1641, ("the oldest account in detail of English thatching," according to Mr. Innocent) thought otherwise, however, and recommended, as the best time for thatching, three weeks or a month before, "yow beginne to cutte grasse," for then the days are long and the barns are empty for sewing, and later in the season it, ". . . will not gette a man heate in a frosty morninge, sittinge on the toppe of an house wheare the winde commeth to him on every side. . . ."[1] Best was evidently of a kindly and considerate nature.

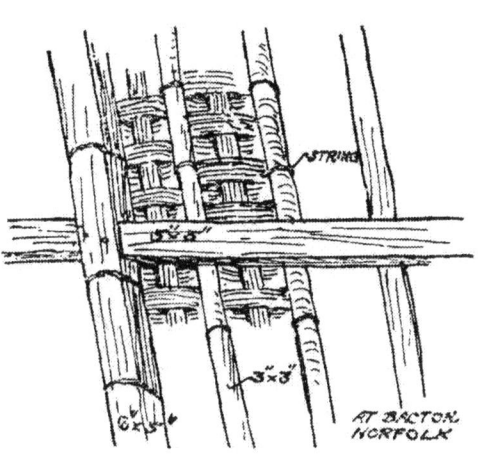

Fig. 35.—Reed plait, instead of laths, tied to rafters under thatched roof, at Bacton, near North Walsham, Norfolk.

There are four ways of securing thatch to roofs, (1) by sewing; (2) by rods laid across it, the rods being tied or sewn to rafters; (3) by thrusting the thatch into or between turves; or (4) by ropes stretched over the surface, crossed at right angles at intervals of 12 inches or 18 inches, weighted down by stones hanging from the ends of the ropes as in the Isle of Man, the Isle of Lewis and in other parts of Scotland and Ireland. This last method is the most

[1] *Ibid*, p. 211, quoting from Best's *Farming Book*, or *Rural Economy in Yorkshire*, pp. 137–148.

M*

primitive, and is neither sightly nor lasting, as the straw ropes decay after about two years.

Laths, nailed to the rafters, were not always used for securing the thatch. Mr. Alfred Powell has sketched an example at Bacton, near North Walsham, Norfolk (Fig. 35) of reed plait, instead of laths, tied to rafters under thatched roof. Wattling is a very ancient method for Bede has recorded the burning of a wattle and thatch roof in the North of England as far back as 642, which must surely be the earliest reference to English roofing materials.[1]

Fig. 36.—Fence at side of Dormer against thatch, at Isle Abbots, near Taunton, Somerset.

The thatch was either tied with withes to the wattling, or pegged to it. After being thus secured the surface was beaten flat and, in the case of straw thatch was combed down with a thatcher's rake. Where the pitch of the rafters is 50 degrees the pitch of the halm or stalk should be about 30 degrees. In this way about ¼ inch of the extremity is exposed to the weather, or, to use Mr. Powell's words ". . . much as the undisturbed fur of some animals in which the tips of the separate hairs alone are visible. . . ."[2]

Reeds, unlike the combing down applied to straw, are knocked up with a tool known as a "legget," and this is used with great effect all over the roof.

Dormers and junctions with chimneys require special

[1] *Ecclesiastical History of the English People*, Book III, Chapter X.
[2] *The Architect's Journal*, Dec. 12, 1923, p. 860.

FEATURES AND DETAILS

care and sound workmanship to resist the weather, otherwise these vulnerable points are bound to give trouble.

Fig. 36 shows an unusual but pleasing feature from Somerset in the form of a shaped wood fence against thatch at the side of a dormer at Isle Abbots, near Taunton, and Fig. 37 indicates, in section, a board fixed to the feet of rafters and projecting over plate so as to lift the thatch over window. This is also in the same village.

Every part of the country, and almost every county, had its own strange terminology and the tools, with their names, also varied considerably, but this aspect of this fascinating subject can best be studied in the *English Dialect Dictionary*.

The choice of Mr. E. Leslie Badham's attractive water-colour of Westham, Pevensey, Sussex (Frontispiece) was made before it was known that the amenities of this beautiful village were threatened by the ill-advised proposal to erect, in close proximity to the Castle ruins, a central slaughter-house for Kent and Sussex Wholesale Butchers and Graziers, Limited, the promoters of the scheme.

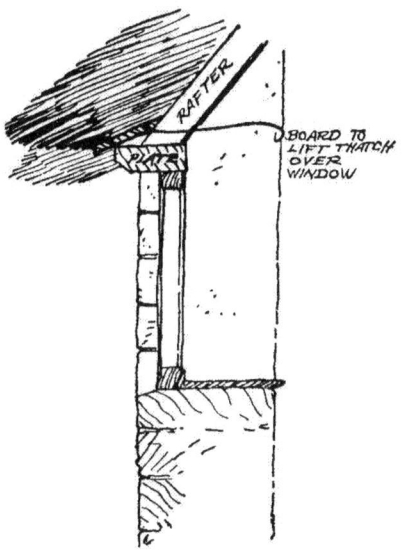

Fig. 37.—Thatch over a window at Isle Abbots, near Taunton, Somerset.

Very natural dismay was thereby created, not only locally, but amongst all lovers of the countryside.

In spite of powerful Press influence, local pressure and the efforts of the ever watchful Council for the Preservation of Rural England, Eastbourne Rural District Council have approved the plans and have so far refused to sanction other plans submitted by the promoters, for an alternative site, to the east of Pevensey, with fewer objections.

The sturdy stone church-tower, of true Sussex type, dominates the picture which was felt to be worthy of colour reproduction and of a place of honour in this book. The hipped and tiled roofs of the cottages, with vertical tile-hanging on the left, and half-timber work with the long low lead-glazed casement windows on the right, form an actual composition which epitomizes in an exceptionally happy manner, many of the regional characteristics that have earned for the South-Eastern counties such a well deserved reputation for unselfconscious and beautiful folk-building.

Fig. 38.

Plate 99

OLD CIDER MILL AT KILCOT, NEWENT, GLOUCESTERSHIRE

THATCHED WALL AT BLEWBURY, NEAR DIDCOT, BERKSHIRE

HERRING-BONE STONE-WALLING AT LEE, NEAR ILFRACOMBE, DEVONSHIRE
(See plate 20, Tintagel old Post Office for another example of dry herring-bone garden walling)

INDEX TO TEXT

A Cotswold Village, by J. Arthur Gibbs, extract from, 12, 13
Aerial views, reference to, 11
Anderson, A. Whitford, F.R.I.B.A., xi
Architects' Journal, 81
Aspect, 2, 3

Badham, E. Leslie, R.B.A., x
Baines, Sir Frank, K.C.V.O., ix
Baker, Sir Herbert, A.R.A., 69
Baldwin, The Rt. Hon. Stanley, M.P., vi, vii, viii
Batsford, Harry, Hon., A.R.I.B.A., ix, xii
Batsford, Messrs. B. T., Ltd., ix, xii
Bay windows, successful and unsuccessful, 53, 54
Best, Henry, 83
Bibury, Purchase by R.S.A. of Arlington Row at, 22, 23
Blacklock, H. H., x
Blight, J. T., 20
Blue Tiles from The Potteries in S. Staffs, 15
Boorde, Dr. Andrew, 2
Bricks, more largely used in E. Anglia owing to lack of stone, than elsewhere at first, 61
Bricks, probably sometimes imported into Eastern Counties owing to proximity of Netherlands, 61
Bricks, too costly (like tiles) for general use, and more so for cottage-building in 15th century, 61
Bricks, effect of Great Fire of London on manufacture of, 61

Bricks, sizes of, 61, 62
Bricks, gap between Roman times and 13th century in the making of, 60, 61
Brick chimneys, comparison between Suffolk and Kent, Surrey and Sussex types, 65, 66
Brick chimneys, how to build, 67
Brick-built cottages, paucity of good old, 60
Brick diapering, 63
Bricks, early scarcity of, 60
Brick earth, effect of oxide of iron in, 62
Brick earth, effect of lime in, 62, 63
Bricks, limited use in Wilts. of, 68
Brick nogging, 34
Brick tumbling, 63
Buckmaster, Mrs. Dorothy, xii
Bull, Edgar R., F.R.P.S., x

Carstone in W. Norfolk, the use of, 62
Casements, wrought iron, 74
Chalk to improve quality of cob and other methods of strengthening, 52, 53
Chalmers, Robert, F.R.P.S., xi
Charles II, King, 79
Characteristics of Old Cottages, 4, 5
Charm of old plastering, reasons for the, 46
Chesterton, G. K., 2
Chequer patterns of flint and stone, 22
Chimney-breasts, advantages of internal, 71
Chimneys, cylindrical, 16, 71, 72

87

INDEX TO TEXT

Chimneys in Somerset and Devon, traditional position of, 16, 21
Cider Mill, reference to illustration of old, 80
Civil War, cottages unchanged since, 6
Clay and cow-dung, the use of, 44
Clay, necessity for the protection of, 50
Clay digging, description of, 50, 51
Clay-lump building, 48, 49
Clay-lump, often mistaken for plastered brickwork, 49
Clay-lump used in Norfolk since 17th century, 50
Clayton, B. C., xi
Clunch used with brick in Cambs., 49
Cob-building, tools used in, 52
Cob-building, method described, 52
Cob-building, reasons for rounded corners, 52
Cob or clem, 20
Cob or clem, necessity for the protection of, 50
Colley Weston slates, 26
Coln Valley above Fairford, 14
Contrast in types referred to, 24
Corbusier, 80
Corder, John S., 63, 64
Cottage-gardens, 78, 79
Council for the Preservation of Rural England, 85
Country Life, 81
County Councils, 2
Cranford, Mrs. Gaskell's, 2
Cowley, Abraham, 79
Cromwell, Oliver, 39
Cruck Construction, 40

Damp-proof course, absence of, 31
Darkening of exposed timbers, a stupid, modern craze and æsthetic mistake, 43
Davie, W. Galsworthy, xii
Destruction of forests, influences of the, 24
Devonshire, the Earl of, 25

Diamond panes, supposed origin of, 76
Domestic Architecture of the Middle Ages, Turner and Parker's, 4
Doors and windows, 3
Doorways, ample width of old, 72
Dormer windows in thatched roofs, 26, 84
Dragon beams, meaning of, 32
Dry-walling, 79
Dwarf-walls or plinths of timber structures, 31
Dyetary of Helth, Dr. Andrew Boorde's, 2

East Anglian timber-framing, examples of, 40
Eastbourne Rural District Council, 85
Eaves, one treatment of, 77, 78
Elizabeth, Queen, 5
Elm-boarding, straight-edged and waney-edged, 58
Elm-boarding, certain disadvantages, 58
Ex-Kaiser, quotation from book by the, 6
External plastering, the reasons for, 33, 43, 46
External plastering, comparison of types, 46
External staircases, 71, 72

Fasteners, ornamental wrought iron casement, 75
Felton, Herbert, F.R.P.S., xi
Fincham, W. H. A., x
Flemish brickmakers, employment of, 62
Flemish influences in design of brick buildings, 63
Flint and brick used for infilling in timber structures, 34, 62
Flints, general use in E. Anglia of, 60
Flint and stone with brick quoins, 68
Floors, 5
Flues, large size of old ones and their disadvantages, 66, 67

INDEX TO TEXT

Foundations often inadequate, 3, 19
Frith and Co., Ltd., F., xi
Furniture, 4, 5, 6

Gardens, 54, 78 79
Gardens, Sir Henry Wotton on, 78
Gardens, Abraham Cowley's little poem on, 79
Garnetting, meaning and advantage of, 70
Gaskell, Mrs. 2
Geological influences, 8, 9, 10
Geological Map of England and Wales, x, 9
Gibbs, J. Arthur, 12, 13, 14
Great Fire of London and its effect on manufacture and use of bricks, 61
Green, W. Curtis, A.R.A., 56, 66, 67

Harrison, William, 5
Harrison, W. J., x
Hepworth, George, xi
Herring-bone brick nogging, reasons for the use of, 34, 38, 39
Herring-bone dry-walling, 79, 80
Herring-bone or zig-zag scratched or pricked plaster patterns, 45
Hertfordshire, example of brick cottages dissimilar to those in Norfolk, etc., 65
Horizontal alternating bands of flint and stone, 22
Horizontality, good example of, 73
Horman, William, 44
Horniman, E. J., x
Hudswell, Percy S., x

Impressed patterns in external plastering, 45
Imrie, G. Blair, 81, 82
Innocent, C. F., 5, 19, 20, 30, 33, 35, 44, 48, 51, 52, 53, 74, 77, 82, 83
Inn sign, wrought iron, 76
Insertion of flint chips in mortar joints, 70

Instructions for thatching, written in 1641, 83
Internal panelling, reasons for the use of, 33
Interlacing squares in scratched plaster, 45
Iron casement-fasteners, wrought, 75
Iron casements, wrought, 74
Iron, wrought, 73–76

James I, King, 78
Jones, Sydney R., x, 8, 9, 68, 69

Kent and Sussex Wholesale Butchers and Graziers, Ltd., 85
Knapped flintwork, 69
Knights of St. John of Jerusalem, 24

Lacing causes of thin square Roman bricks, 60
Landlords, 7
Langley, Batty, and pargetting, 44
Lead-glazing, 76, 77
Leicestershire, lack of good old cottages in, 26
Lime in brick earth, effect of, 62, 63,
Limewash as a waterproofing medium and how best made, 67
Lingering tradition in remote places, 7
Lloyd, Nathaniel, O.B.E., F.S.A., xi, 46, 59, 62
London Prices, of 1750, Batty Langley's, 44
Loss of original windows, how buildings are marred by, 15

Maclagan, Eric, C.B.E., F.S.A., x
Magpie work, 35, 73
Material, commonsense use of, 68, 69
May, E. J., F.R.I.B.A., xi, 36–39
Mediæval shop-front, at Lavenham, uncovered in recent years, 41
Menzies, G. K., M.A., ix
Messent, Claude, J. W., 50
Ministry of Health, 2
Models, 3
Modern conveniences, lack of, 6

INDEX TO TEXT

Modern requirements
Mompesson, Rev. William, 25
Mompesson, Mrs. W., 26
Morris, William, vi, 3, 14
Mortise and tenon used from the earliest times, 31
Mud walls, durability due to coating of plaster, 44

National Trust (for Places of Historic Interest or Natural Beauty), 21
Nineteenth century as worst period of brick-making and brick-laying, 61

Office of Works, His Majesty's, 22
Old methods of building, J. J. Stevenson's reference to, 7
Ordnance Survey Office, Director General of, xi
Ornamental lead-glazing, 77
Ornamental wrought iron casement fasteners, 75
Ox-hair used to strengthen plaster, 43
Oxide of iron, effect in brickmaking of, 62

Panel filling in timber structures, the various kinds of, 33
Pantiles, common in Norfolk, Lincs. and Yorks., 63
Peasant's House, Piers Plowman's, 4
Pinners, meaning of, 70
Pitch of roofs, differences in, 14, 15
Pitcher, Sydney, F.R.P.S., xi
Place-names, the attractiveness of many, 8, 22
Plague in Derbyshire in 1665, 25
Planning of old cottages, 4, 23
Plans of villages, 11
Plaster, reasons for the good quality and toughness of old, 43
Plowman, Piers, 4
Powell, Alfred H., xi, 7, 28–31, 70, 79–81, 83–86
Porch-roofs ingeniously thatched, 67
Post-and-pan construction, 34; why so called, 38

Pricked plaster patterns, 44
Projecting upper storeys, supposed reasons for, 32, 33

Radwinter, William Harrison, Rector of, 5
Reconditioning, 2
Rectangular panes, cheaper than diamond panes, 77
Reed-thatching, 81, 82
Removal of hair from hides for plastering, old and new methods compared, 44
Renaissance influence, 73
Road-scrapings, 44
Rogers, Professor Thorold, 61
Roof-construction, example of, 41
Roofing slates and stones, 15
Royal Academy of Arts, x
Royal Commission on Historical Monuments, x
Royal Photographic Society of Great Britain, ix
Royal Society of Arts, vii, viii, 23
Rural District Councils, 2

Saltpetre men, 5
Saxon kings in Cornwall, gathering of seven, 21
Scalloped fan-patterns on scratched or pricked plaster, 45
Scott, Thomas H. B., F.R.P.S., x
Scratched plaster patterns, 44
Securing thatch to roof, different methods of, 83, 84
Sheep-farming in the Cotswolds, 13
Ship-building, timber for the use of, 27
Slate-hanging, 71
Society for the Protection of Ancient Buildings, 20
Speculators, 1
Spinning gallery, example of, 71, 72
Spit-and-dab work, 53
Staircases, 3
Stanley, Rev. Thomas, 25
Stevenson, J. J., 7

INDEX TO TEXT

Stickwork, Essex, 44
Stone used in Cornish cottages, the large size of, 19, 20
Stone foundations for cob walls, the importance of, 51, 52
Stone surrounds to doors and windows, 73
Straw used for toughening clay, 34
Stripping of external plastering, the folly of, 43
Studio Magazine, the Editor of, x
Swann, Rev. Sidney, x
Swithland slates, 26

Tapestry, origin of the use of, 33
Tar, depressing effect of too great a use of, 50
Tarred brick plinths or dwarf-walls, 49
Taunt, xii
Taylor, Will F., xi
Tempering, 51
Thatch, details of thatching; methods, tools used, etc.; pros and cons of, 80–83
Thatched walling, 80
Tile-hanging chiefly peculiar to S.E. counties, 55
Tile-hanging, effectiveness of, as a means of protection from driving rain, 55
Tile-hanging, patterned, 56
Tiles, the size of, 56
Tiles when first made much more expensive than thatch, 56
Timber-framing, methods of, 28–33
Timber-yielding districts, 27, 28
Topiary work in a cottage-garden, 54
Troup, F. W., F.S.A., F.R.I.B.A., 49
Tudors, The, 13
Turner and Parker, 4
Two-roomed cottage, plan of, 23

Ugliness of large sheets of glass in windows, 16

Vandalism at Pevensey, threatened, 85, 86
Victoria and Albert Museum, x, 74–76
Village crosses, 14
Village plans, 12, 13
Vulgaria, Quotations from Wm. Horman's, 44

Warrewyk, Michael, 62
Wars of the Roses, some cottages unchanged since, 6
Wattle-and-daub, 33
Warwickshire timber-framing, 36, 37, etc.
Weather-boarding, tar used for, 50, 58
Weather-boarding of oak, or elm, 57
Weather-boarding, once commonly used for windmills and watermills, 58
Weather-boarding, painted white, 58
Week-end cottages, 1
Whitewashed brickwork, effectiveness of, 67
Whitewash, the softening effect of repeated applications, 45
William the Conqueror, 13
Windows of different types, 73
Window-mullions in Derbyshire, unmoulded, 15
Windows, sliding, 26
Winchester College War Memorial, the use of decorative flint in
Witchit, 51
Woodley, Arthur J., x
Wotton, Sir Henry, v, 3, 78
Wrought iron, 73–76
Wrought iron inn-sign, 76

Yellow bricks, where made and used, 62
Yews, clipped, 54

www.ingramcontent.com/pod-product-compliance
Lightning Source LLC
Chambersburg PA
CBHW060951230426
43665CB00015B/2156